ISLAM IN...
Series Editor: Malise Ruthven

The '*Islam in...*' series explores the different cultural political and social manifestations of Islam in different contexts. Each volume represents both an investigation into Muslim life in that country, and a contribution to our understanding of the wider questions surrounding the relationships between Islam and politics, global and local influences, and minorities and the state.

Books in the series:
Islam in America, Jonathan Curiel
Islam in Saudi Arabia, David Commins

Jonathan Curiel is a former staff writer for the *San Francisco Chronicle*, whose work has also appeared in the *Columbia Journalism Review*, Salon.com and the *LA Times*. He is the author of *Al' America: Travels through America's Arab and Islamic Roots* (2008).

'Finally, an ethically disinterested observer's clear, concise, and comprehensive survey of the American Muslim community. *Islam in America* is a fascinating and long overdue book about the faith and its followers that have been part of the tapestry of America from its inception.'

Hamza Yusuf, President & Co-Founder,
Zaytuna College, Berkeley, CA

'So many years after 9/11, the gulf between Muslims and non-Muslims in the United States remains depressingly wide. We still need a much better and more nuanced understanding of Islam, especially after the tragic events in Paris. Jonathan Curiel is therefore to be commended for giving us this closely-argued and highly readable book which - as both labor of love and much needed antidote to prejudice and misunderstanding - is intended to close the gap.'

Akbar Ahmed, Ibn Khaldun Chair of Islamic Studies and
Professor of International Relations, American University,
Washington, DC, and formerly Pakistan's
High Commissioner in London

'*Islam in America* offers a remarkably original and readable narrative of the history of Islam and Muslims in America. Jonathan Curiel here reveals a side of American Muslim culture that is as old as America itself.'

Jamal Dajani, independent journalist-host, **Arab Talk Radio**

ISLAM IN
AMERICA

JONATHAN CURIEL

I.B. TAURIS
LONDON · NEW YORK

Published in 2015 by
I.B.Tauris & Co. Ltd
London • New York
www.ibtauris.com

ISBN: HB 978 1 84885 598 4
PB 978 1 84885 599 1
eISBN: 978 0 85773 810 3

A full CIP record for this book is available from the British Library
A full CIP record is available from the Library of Congress

Library of Congress Catalog Card Number: available

Typeset in 12/15pt Adobe garamond Pro by JCS Publishing Services Ltd,
www.jcs-publishing.co.uk

Printed and bound in Great Britain by T.J. International, Padstow, Cornwall

Contents

Foreword

Despite the atrocity of 11 September 2001, when the Muslim terrorists who attacked the World Trade Center in New York and the Pentagon near Washington inflicted the heaviest death toll on the American mainland since the end of the Civil War, Islam is alive and prospering in the United States. As *Newsweek* magazine commented in 2007, 'Muslim Americans represent the most affluent, integrated, politically engaged Muslim community in the Western world.'[1] Muslim success is closely related to the upward mobility of migrants from East and South Asia who arrived in the United States after 1965, when President Johnson passed the Hart–Celler Act, repealing immigration quotas based on national diversity within the US. By 1990, immigrants from South Asia were well ahead of other groups in terms of income and educational attainments, with the highest proportion of newcomers working in management and professions such as medicine. Though Muslims from South Asia may not have exceeded the numbers of immigrants with Hindu or Sikh backgrounds, the anthropologist Karen Leonard suggests that the general ethos was such as to make them seem a 'particularly privileged group' with a reputation for being 'model immigrants', making them 'conspicuous and powerful in Muslim American discourse and politics'.[2] Often classified as 'white' rather than Asian-Americans or Muslim-Americans, they fared better than immigrants from Arab countries, who were more likely to be victims of prejudice.

This generally rosy picture, of course, does not apply to everyone. At the lower end of the social scale it is estimated that some 15 percent of prisoners incarcerated in US correctional institutions (350,000 out of approximately 2.3 million) are Muslims, a percentage that is vastly disproportionate to the Muslim-American population, even going by the largest of the available estimates. (In their 2007 survey the Pew Organization placed Islam behind Judaism and Buddhism as the third largest US religion after Christianity, with 0.6 percent of the population). The incarceration figure for federal prisons generally is roughly consistent with that for the state of New York, where anthropologist Robert Dannin found that Muslims – most of them converts – represented more than 16 percent of a prison population of 70,000, and almost one-third of the African-Americans incarcerated by the state.[3]

Dannin, who devoted many months to researching in New York's prisons, found that Islam had a remarkably mitigating effect as an alternative to the brutal culture of incarceration. 'Prison', he explained, 'is a bizarre and violent "university" for those who reach maturity behind bars', where the brutality and corruption of the streets in the downtown ghettos are vastly concentrated. Far from teaching the skills that will enable an inmate to lead a law-abiding life after his release, prison effectively destroys his sense of personal integrity by methods that include 'physical brutality, psychological manipulation and frequent homosexual rape'.[4]

Conversion to Islam, Dannin found, allowed the prisoner to use his right to freedom of worship to 'circumscribe an autonomous zone whose perimeter cannot officially be contested'. The Muslim convert's Islamic identity and membership of the world-wide *ummah* (community) meant a 'fresh start, symbolized by a new name, modifications of his physical appearance and an emphasis on prayer'. The prison mosque became an alternative focus of authority, while the Muslim's cell could be 'recognized by the absence of photographic images and the otherwise ubiquitous centerfold pin-ups of naked women'.[5] The Islamic regime's strict opposition to homosexuality acted as a 'counter-disciplinary resistance' to the dominant hierarchies of prison life, where 'sexual possession, domination and submission represent forms of "hard currency".' Muslim prisoners were better placed than others to resist invasive body searches ostensibly used to find drugs, but actually employed to humiliate inmates. They claimed, plausibly enough, that since their religion forbade alcohol and narcotics, there was no reason to probe their orifices. Interestingly, Dannin also suggested that the Islamic regime extended to the world outside the prison walls. So fierce was the reputation of the prison enclaves where Islamic *sharia* law was applied, if unofficially, that even the most ruthless urban drug dealers carefully avoided harming any Muslim man, woman or child, for fear of the retribution they might face in the more than likely event of them finding themselves incarcerated.[6]

Jonathan Curiel, in this engaging and accessible account of Islam in America, did not have Dannin's access to prison or prisoners, but his findings generally show how a faith that provides discipline, structure, and hope for a notoriously deprived underclass can also appeal to one of the country's most dynamic rising elites. Despite surveys revealing that some 43 percent of Americans feel 'a little' prejudice against Muslims (as compared with 18 percent against Christians and 15 percent against Jews and Buddhists), America is one of the leading countries for conversion to Islam, with some 30,000 conversions per year, including many Hispanics and Anglos in addition to African-Americans. Prejudice experienced by Muslims since 9/11 clearly remains an obstacle, with converts sometimes concealing their religion for fear of losing their jobs or social connections. Public attitudes, however, are likely to become more positive because of the constitutional protections accorded to religion. Thanks to the 'wall of separation' between church and state erected by its founding fathers, America is unusually inviting and accessible to all faith traditions.

In registering the echoes of Islamic memory in Africa brought by slaves, Curiel charts the evolution of Islam as a separatist, even racist, movement in the early twentieth century before contact with the Islamic mainstream demonstrated that the faith ultimately transcends all types of ethnic or social particularism. Malcolm X, the iconic model of American Islam, adopted the path of millions of his predecessors (ranging from Turkic tribes of Inner Asia to diverse communities in equatorial Africa) when he abandoned the separatist ideology of the Nation of Islam and joined the Sunni mainstream led by Warith al-Deen Muhammad. Warith al-Deen (formerly Wallace) was the son of Elijah Muhammad, an eclectic quasi-prophet who combined an array of elements in his bizarrely racist theology. Drawn from popular American culture, these included the millennial eschatologies shared by Baptists and Adventists, Gnostic ideas of salvation imparted via secret codes or other versions of specialist knowledge, alongside echoes of the Kabbala, Identity Christianity, Scientology, and Mormonism. The rump of Elijah Muhammad's movement, led by the ailing Louis Farrakhan, still has some 50,000 members. The journey of Warith al-Deen and Malcolm X from eclecticism to orthodoxy revealed how the centripetal pull of majoritarian Islam has an inherent tendency to overcome the peculiar genesis of a local tradition, represented in this case by white-on-black slavery. The religious mainstreaming of American Islam is matched by a degree of political mainstreaming. There are now two Muslim members of Congress. One of them, Keith Ellision, elected in 2007, made constitutional history by swearing his oath of allegiance on a copy of the Quran owned by Thomas Jefferson.

There remain of course many obstacles and difficulties before Islam is fully integrated into the American pantheon of faiths. As Catholics found in the nineteenth century, when Irish immigrants faced the rage of Protestant nativism, and Jewish immigrants would find when meeting social prejudice, public acceptance takes time. In campaigning for election and re-election, President Barack Obama had to assert his Christian credentials against a barrage of allegations – based on his Kenyan paternity and middle-name Hussein – that he was a crypto-Muslim. Curiel relates that during Obama's first campaign for the presidency aides prevented two Muslim women from standing on the candidate's podium because they feared their head-coverings would send the wrong signal to the audience and television viewers.

Populist anxieties may be stoked by figures deliberately inflated by both Muslim organizations and their opponents. As Curiel explains (on pp. 66–7), estimates of the number of Muslim adherents vary hugely, from the 1.3 million of the American Religious Identification Survey, through the Pew Organization's 2.35 million, to the six to nine million suggested by some US Muslim organizations. Precise estimates are prevented by a number of factors: the official US census does not ask or register religious affiliation, so figures depend on who is doing the counting, with political–cultural agendas (whether pro- or anti-Muslim) enlisted to inflate or deflate the figures. Then there are the inevitable uncertainties about religious identities and affiliations: many Muslims living in the US and other Western countries do not attend a mosque or participate in religious observances such as the Ramadan fast or the Feast of Sacrifice (Eid al-Adha). Some may choose to assimilate, changing first names such as Ya'coub to Jack. Fareed to Fred, Ali or Alauddin to Al, or Nasreen to Nancy. Yvonne Haddad's 1987 study estimated mosque attendance at between 10 and 20 percent, way behind the 40 percent figure for Christian churches. However the figures are arrived at, there can be little doubt that American Islam is growing, both as a marker of identity (with American-born Muslims identifying themselves as 'Muslim-Americans' rather than 'Pakistani-Americans' or 'African-Americans' who happened to be Muslim), and in religious observance. Curiel points out that the number of mosques has steadily increased, from 1,209 in 2000 to 2,106 in 2011, an increase of well over 70 percent. Mosque building is matched by a small but consistent increase in attendance.

Formal observance by acknowledged adherents is only a part of this picture. As Curiel points out (pp. 70–1), the Islamic mystical tradition of Sufism has long been growing in popularity, exemplified by the success of Coleman Barks' verse translation of Jalaludin Rumi, which has sold some half million copies since its first publication. Not all Sufi adherents, or people who attend Sufi ceremonies or *dhikrs*, regard themselves as Muslims. The spiritual ideas of Rumi, Ibn Arabi, and other Sufi masters are inherently appealing in the culture that proved receptive to Transcendentalists and Unitarians, to the poetry of Walt Whitman and essays of Ralph Waldo Emerson. Sufism apart, even mainstream, orthodox Islam is now being indigenized in the US: witness the impressive efforts by women scholars, such as Leila Ahmed and Laleh Bakhtiar, and activists such as Amina Wuddud, to reassert the feminine in Islamic tradition and practice. In a globalizing culture dominated by the internet (itself a product of American technological hegemony) these initiatives are bound to have a major impact on the Muslim world at large. American Islam is shaking the tradition's received certainties, offering new visions and challenges at a time of deep crisis, caused in part by the exercise of American power in the Muslim heartlands.

Malise Ruthven

Preface

Islam's Growing Presence in America

The road into Moscow, Idaho takes visitors straight to the city center, to a thoroughfare whose name embodies small-town America: Main Street. It is Main Street where all of Moscow's most historic and popular storefronts are located – where people go to eat breakfast, lunch, and dinner (favored by students: the A&W restaurant, which offers cheeseburgers with '100 percent US beef'); where they buy clothing, books, and high-end gifts; and where they take in movies, concerts, and (at bars like the Corner Club, which advertises '32-ounce tubs of beer') televised sporting events. If there's something important in Moscow, it inevitably finds its way to Main Street. In February 2010, that 'something' was a message on the front door of the Moscow Chamber of Commerce Visitor Center, at 411 South Main Street, in the form of a poster that read, 'Immigration is an American Experience' and 'Acceptance is an Idaho Value.'

One hundred years ago, Moscow's residents were mostly white and Christian, but today the city of 20,000 residents is a mix of ethnicities and religions. A few minutes' walk from Main Street is the Islamic Center of Moscow, where the city's Muslims go to pray, hold community meetings, and share information about such things as buying halal food and donating to Islamic causes. The center is a converted house from the mid 1900s that is painted white and – from the outside – still looks like a typical mid twentieth-century house, except for the words that are spelt out in dark letters, 'Islamic Center of Moscow'.

'Idaho has two mosques – Boise and here,' one of the Islamic center's members, Adam Frey, says to me as he stands in front of the building. 'Alaska is building one. Montana has built one. Now, all 50 states are covered.'

That milestone – having every American state with a mosque – took less than 100 years, stretching from the time that US Muslims built their first houses of worship in the 1920s, in such small towns as Highland Park, Michigan, and Ross, North Dakota. Mosques, which number more than 2,000 in the United States,[1] are one of many gauges of Islam's growing reach in America. Between 2 million and 9 million Muslims now live in the United States – a dramatic increase from the estimated 200,000–500,000 Muslims who lived in the country in 1960.[2]

Almost 25 percent of American Muslims are converts[3] – people like Adam Frey, who decided to leave the United States' most popular faith (Christianity) for one of its fastest-growing ones. Every day, about 90 Americans convert to Islam, according to *The American Mosque 2011*, a survey done by a bloc of organizations that included the Council on American–Islamic Relations, which is a political advocacy group, and the Association of Statisticians of American Religious Bodies.[4] Few other countries in the world have such a high rate of conversion to the Muslim faith.

Since 2000, American Muslims have accomplished a number of 'firsts', including having the first Muslim elected to Congress (Keith Ellison, in 2007); the first Muslim to win the Miss USA beauty contest (Rima Fakih in 2010); and the first *hijab*-wearing Muslim woman to advise a US president (Dalia Mogahed, appointed in 2009 to the White House Office of Faith-Based and Neighborhood Partnerships).

The year 2010 also saw the opening of the first Muslim liberal arts college in the United States – Zaytuna College, located in Berkeley, California, where its faculty is led by a quartet of leading Muslim academics, including Imam Zaid Shakir, a prominent African-American scholar; and Sheikh Hamza Yusuf, a Greek-American convert to Islam. In 2009, Yusuf was named 'the Western world's most influential Islamic scholar' in *The 500 Most Influential Muslims*, an annual work published by the Royal Islamic Strategic Studies Centre in Amman, Jordan.[5] At Zaytuna College's 2010 convocation, prominent US Muslims and scholars came from around the country to give their blessings, including Virginia Gray Henry, a descendant of American founding father Patrick Henry, whose 'Give me liberty, or give me death' speech in 1775 was a crucial event in US history. The appearance by Henry, who is a publisher, author, organizer, and filmmaker living in Louisville, Kentucky, was noted with pride: 'This is a historic and momentous occasion,' said Hatem Bazian, a Palestinian-American lecturer at both Zaytuna College and the University of California at Berkeley.

Bazian, Yusuf, Shakir, Henry, Frey, Ellison, Fakih, and Mogahed represent the past, present, and future of American Islam. Their histories are histories of immigration, conversion, multiple ethnicities, multiple levels of faith, and multiple levels of public acceptance. In November 2006, shortly after Ellison won a primary election in the Midwest state of Minnesota that solidified his election to Congress, he gave a national TV interview to Glenn Beck, a conservative host who said that Ellison's religion made him 'nervous'. Beck then told Ellison, 'What I feel like saying is, "Sir, prove to me that you are not working with our enemies." And I know you're not. I'm not accusing you of being an enemy, but that's the way I feel, and I think a lot of Americans will feel that way.'[6]

From its beginnings in America, Islam has felt like an 'enemy religion' for many Americans. In May 1788 – a month before the US Constitution was ratified – a prominent newspaper in the US state of Connecticut editorialized, 'The faith of Mahomet, wherever it is established, is unified with despotic power.'[7] Three years earlier, though, George Washington said he would welcome Muslims to his own estate in Virginia – provided they were 'good workmen'.[8] And America's second-most prominent founding father, Thomas Jefferson, had a copy of the Quran in his own library, studied Arabic (which he taught himself to read),[9] and – like Washington – said America welcomed people of all religions, including those of the Abrahamic faiths.

In fact, the foundation for Islam's long-term acceptance was established by the country's founding fathers, who recognized it as a faith of widespread importance, even as they described Muslims as 'Mahometans' – i.e. people who follow the Prophet Muhammad. Jefferson, the main author of the Declaration of Independence ('We hold these truths to be self-evident, that all men are created equal'), cited Islam when he said freedom of religion was a sacred tenet of America's vaunted principles. Jefferson was an Enlightenment-influenced Deist who disregarded the emphasis that Christianity (and other religions) placed on miracles, and he said no particular faith should be prescribed for America's citizens, writing of a 1785 Virginia law guaranteeing religious expression that it was 'meant to comprehend, within the mantle of its protection, the Jew and the Gentile, the Christian and the Mahometan, the Hindoo, and Infidel of every denomination'.[10]

In 1797, the United States signed a treaty with the Tripoli government in North Africa that stated that America held Muslim nations in high esteem – and that America was a country of free choice in religion. The overture read: 'As the Government of the United States of America is not, in any sense, founded on the Christian religion – as it has in itself no character of enmity against the laws, religion, or tranquility, of Mussulmen (Muslims) – and as the said States never entered into any war or act of hostility against any Mahometan (Muslim) nation, it is declared by the parties that no pretext arising from religious opinions shall ever produce an interruption of the harmony existing between the two countries.'[11]

A few years later, America was at war with Tripoli, and American enmity and distrust of Islam – and of Muslims – would reach a feverish pitch. Islam was incompatible with America's democratic system, Alexis de Tocqueville implied after crisscrossing the United States in 1831. Writing in *Democracy in America*, de Tocqueville said Islam as practiced in Muslim countries insinuated itself in every aspect of its adherents' lives and cultures and thus 'will never long predominate in a cultivated and democratic age'.[12] America's relationship with Islam has always fluctuated and – paradoxically, perhaps – has always led to periods of greater understanding of the religion and a greater recognition that America's religious and philosophical traditions share commonalities with some of Islam's principal beliefs. In the mid nineteenth century, for example, American Transcendentalists – led by Ralph Waldo

Emerson – said the Muslim faith as embodied by Hafiz, Saadi, and other Sufi poets mirrored the ideals of Transcendentalism, which laid out ethical behavior that put people in harmony with their natural surroundings. Emerson, who studied Islam and its connection to Sufi poetry, lauded the religion and said that one of America's key's obligations was 'to take in the immigrant'[13] – views that would presage the increased immigration that, in the mid twentieth century, dramatically boosted the number of American Muslims. Black nationalism was another key factor in the trajectory of American Islam, as was the political emergence that led to Ellison's post-9/11 election to the US Congress.

When Ellison, a Democrat, went through his ceremonial swearing-in in 2007, he put his hand on Jefferson's Quran, using the Muslim holy book instead of the Bible that is traditionally used for such Congressional events. For Ellison, the swearing-in was a chance to show Islam's historic reach in the United States, but for Virgil Goode, a Republican Senator from Virginia, Ellison's act was an affront, with Goode warning his constituents that, 'in the next century we will have many more Muslims in the United States if we do not adopt strict immigration policies.'[14]

The story of Islam in America continues to evolve, continues to be tinged with controversy, especially in the wake of the 9/11 terrorist attacks, which polarized Americans' views of Muslims and their religion – unfairly, say US followers of Islam. Sitting in a Moscow, Idaho café located one block from Main Street, members of the Islamic Center of Moscow say their peaceable presence in one of America's remotest, least-populated states – a state with a history of white-supremacy groups – shows that their religion has been accepted by the American public. The Islamic Center of Moscow is in a tree-lined neighborhood of student housing and car dealers, with foot traffic comprising people on their way to and from Main Street.

'People around the mosque know that Muslims are people like everybody,' says Sherif El-Badawy, an engineer from Egypt who is doing a post-doctoral stint at the University of Idaho in Moscow. 'There is no problem to be a neighbor to Muslims. A mosque brings people everyday to pray. People see people worship. And if you worship, usually that means you're a good person. You're trying to be good. You're trying to stick to good deeds. This makes [neighbors] feel, "These people are OK."'

It's not as simple as that, of course. As Bazian points out, the story of Islam in America 'is very complex. It does not lend itself to a neat representation, with a simple line of demarcation.' The zig-zags of American Islam have ultimately led to places like Moscow, Idaho and Berkeley, California – places that are on the opposite side of the country from where America was founded; places where the mosques are peopled by a patchwork of cultures, languages, and religious identities. Sunnis mix with Shiites; African-Americans mix with Asian-Americans; white Americans with Hispanic-Americans. Bazian argues that: 'American Muslims, along with other peoples in this country, are the new face of America in the 21st century: racially and ethnically diverse; culturally open; globally aware; and multi-lingual.'

If that is true, then American Muslims have come full circle. In the years before the founding of America, Islam was publicly marginalized, and Muslims were barely visible as citizens. In 1701, for example, the prominent Puritan minister Cotton Mather, who lived in the Boston area, wrote that Americans 'are afar off, in a Land, which never had (that I ever heard of) one Mahometan breathing in it'.[15]

If Mather had lived in the American south, he would have met Muslims. They worked as slaves on plantations, forcibly taken from their original homes in West Africa. The story of Islam in America really begins in the south, with the slave trade that brought thousands of Muslims to the shores of Louisiana, Mississippi, and other states that formed the burgeoning land that would become the United States of America. These southern slaves formed the roots of American Islam, the roots of America itself.

1 Slavery and the Struggle to Maintain Belief

American Islam, 1619–1865

At first, he was forced to work the tobacco fields. Then it was tending cattle. Four thousand miles from his home in West Africa, where he was born into a noble family of devout Muslims, Ayuba Suleiman Ibrahima Diallo was reduced to doing manual labor as a slave on an American plantation. Speaking no English, he was bonded to a Maryland man, Alexander Tolsey, who purchased Diallo from a slave broker. Tolsey called him 'Job', an anglicization of Diallo's first name. 'Job ben Solomon' was Diallo's complete slave name. The year was 1731, and Diallo was one of tens of thousands of slaves toiling in the American colonies. With no access to a mosque or other formal house of worship, Diallo maintained his prayer rituals by doing what other Muslim slaves did: prostrating himself in the open, often amid the trees and pathways that surrounded his slave quarters. Diallo would also go to the woods on Tolsey's plantation in Kent Island, but even this became problematic, as Diallo recalled in his 1734 memoirs, which were written in the third person by Thomas Bluett, an attorney who befriended Diallo:

Job would often leave the Cattle, and withdraw into the Woods to pray; but a white Boy frequently watched him, and whilst he was at his Devotion would mock him, and throw Dirt in his Face. This very much disturbed Job, and added to his other Misfortunes; all which were increased by his Ignorance of the English Language, which prevented his complaining, or telling his Case to any Person about him.[1]

Muslims numbered upwards of 20 percent of African slaves brought to America.[2] In 1700, about 25,000 African slaves were in the American colonies.[3] By 1750, the number had risen to about 250,000,[4] and by the American Revolution in 1776 it was about 500,000.[5] Muslims slaves weren't allowed full religious freedom. They were pressured to convert to Christianity, put under conditions that discouraged display of their original faith, and otherwise marginalized – they were kept from organizing anything approaching mass prayers or public services. Still, their presence in America gave them the distinction of being the continent's first viable Muslim population.

Though Muslims had made their way to America almost from the time that Europeans claimed the territory in the fifteenth and sixteenth centuries, their numbers were few. In the 1530s, for example, a Moroccan-Muslim slave named Esteban explored what is now the American south. And crypto-Muslims from Spain – supposed Christians who hid their true faith to circumvent Spain's prohibition against Muslims going to the New World – made their way to the shores of America soon after Christopher Columbus' historic voyages. For all intents and purposes, though, Islam was non-existent in America until West African slaves like Diallo were taken by force and put on ships for the weeks-long passage across the Atlantic Ocean.

In West Africa, Diallo had formally studied Islam and, according to one account, had 'assisted his father in the capacity of Imam'.[6] In addition to Wolof and other African languages, Diallo knew how to read and write Arabic. In fact, Diallo's religious bearing helped him in the summer of 1731, after he had fled Kent Island and was caught and imprisoned in Kent County, where – in his cell – he 'was observed to use prostrations at regular periods of the day, and to repeat sentences with great solemnity and earnestness.'[7] Diallo's behavior attracted onlookers, including Bluett, who would help Diallo obtain Tolsey's forgiveness. A short time later, with Tolsey's permission, Diallo wrote a letter (in Arabic) to his father that was eventually seen by an influential British official, James Oglethorpe, who bought Diallo's release – leading to Diallo's return to West Africa, and the publication of Diallo's memoir, *Some Memories of the Life of Job, the Son of the Solomon High Priest of Boonda in Africa; Who Was a Slave about Two Years in Maryland; and Afterwards Being Brought to England, Was Set Free, and Sent to His Native Land in the Year 1734.*

Diallo was the first Muslim slave in America to achieve national and international prominence. He was also an exception: The majority of African slaves in America – Muslim and non-Muslim – spent years and years in miserable conditions on southern plantations and lands, never returning to West Africa or even coming close. Those who retained their Islamic beliefs did so against great odds. Slave-owners continuously proselytized about Christianity. Diallo and other Muslim slaves were given Bibles in Arabic and told the books contained the true word of God – and were then rewarded with respect and privileges if they converted.

This pattern of coercion continued until the last days of slavery in 1865 and helped succeed in snuffing out any serious transference of Islam as a religion among African-American slaves and their progeny. It could not, however, completely eradicate the presence of Islam among the slave population, and there was a begrudging tolerance – if not outright acceptance – for Muslims if they were valuable workers or somehow considered of aristocratic lineage. In the mid 1800s, for example, on Sapelo Island in the state of Georgia, Bilali Mohammed – a practicing Muslim – was in charge of a plantation's other slaves. So entrusted was Mohammed by plantation owner Thomas Spalding, he was given arms during the war of 1812, to fight any British soldiers who stormed Spalding's portion of the island.

Born and raised in what is now northern Guinea, Mohammed spoke and wrote Arabic, owned a Quran, was reported to pray toward Mecca three times a day, use a prayer rug and prayer beads, and wore the kind of fez that religious Muslims wore in eighteenth-century West Africa. Before his death in 1859, Mohammed gave a 13-page Arabic manuscript he had written to a Georgian minister, Francis Robert Goulding, that described the proper Islamic way to do ablutions for prayer, and detailed legal guidelines that pious Muslims should follow.

To his offspring, Mohammed emphasized a Muslim upbringing, and gave several daughters Muslim names, including Medina and Fatima. One daughter, Margaret, wore a Muslim headdress during her life, and Mohammed's great-grandchildren were able to recall the family's Islamic heritage in the 1930s. Using unlearned, phonetic English, Mohammed's great-grandcousin Shadrach 'Shad' Hall told interviewers from the US Works Progress Administration that his grandmother Hester (another of Mohammed's daughters) and her offspring and cousins still followed some rituals of Islam, including the use of Muslim prayer beads. 'Hestuh an all ub um sho pray on duh bead,' Hall, who also lived on Sapelo Island, said in words first published in the 1940 book *Drums and Shadows*. 'Dey weah duh string uh beads on dud wais. Sometime duh sring on duh neck. Dey pray at sun-up and face duh sun on duh knees an bow tuh it tree times, kneelin on a lill mat.'[8]

Later descendants of Bilali Mohammed converted to Christianity, and the island's churches testify to the lasting influence of the dominant faith, but Cornelia Walker Bailey, Mohammed's great-great-great-great-granddaughter, says there are vestiges of Islamic influence on Sapelo Island – in the churches, where men and women sit on separate sides by tradition; in the graves of former slaves that face Mecca; even in the name Bailey, which some historians believe is a reworking of the name Bilali, which itself comes from Islam's first *muezzin* (an Islamic religious reciter), who was named Bilali.

'History changes things,' Bailey, a long-time resident of Sapelo Island, once told me. 'Things become something different from what they started out as.'[9]

During the slave years of the antebellum south, Islam was handed down to new generations – if it was handed down at all – as an 'inwardly directed' religion,[10] to quote historian Michael Gomez, author of the 2005 work, *Black Crescent: The Experience and Legacy of African Muslims in the Americas*. Even conversions of non-Muslims to Islam occurred during this period, but as Gomez reminds his readers, the Muslim community had no infrastructure – no network of mosques, no network of schools, no real connection to the worldwide ummah – to sustain itself. Islam, he writes, 'was an internal affair, steered away from non-Muslims'.[11]

Mohammed's manuscript, written with diacritics (the markings signifying letters' vowel sounds), is one of several significant documents written in Arabic by Muslim slaves in America. The most prominent is an autobiography penned in

1831 by Omar ibn Said, a Muslim slave in North Carolina. The 15-page manuscript – completed when Said would have been in his early sixties – starts with the 67th *surah* of the Quran, *Al-Mulk* ('dominion' or 'ownership'), which begins, 'In the Name of God, most merciful, most gracious', and continues, 'Blessed be He in Whose hands is the Kingdom, and who is Almighty.'[12] Theoretically, Said had converted to Christianity during his 60 years as a slave in the American south, and he regularly attended church services, but his autobiography – even while it lauded Christianity and Jesus Christ – seemed to refute his conversion while upholding the Muslim faith he had studied as a scholar in his native West Africa. The biggest clue was *Al-Mulk*, which implies that only God (Allah) can determine people's fate or faith. Said did profess his admiration of Jesus Christ, and referred to his Muslim life in the past tense:

> When I was a Mohammedan I prayed thus: 'Thanks be to God, Lord of all worlds, the merciful the gracious, Lord of the day of Judgment, thee we serve, on thee we call for help. Direct us in the right way, the way of those on whom thou hast had mercy, with whom thou hast not been angry and who walk not in error. Amen.' But now I pray 'Our Father, etc.,' in the words of our Lord Jesus the Messiah.[13]

Said, though, was playing the 'in-between game',[14] professing enough Christianity to pass as a convert without denying Islam, according to Ala Alryyes, an associate professor of comparative literature at Yale University, who did a new translation of Said's manuscript in 2000. Said died in 1864, rejecting offers from American missionaries to return to his native land as a convert to Christianity. He was born in Futa Toro, in what is now northern Senegal, to a family of religious Muslims. In 1807, at the age of 37, Said (whose last name has also been spelled 'Sayyid' and 'Saeed' by historians and Islamic scholars) was captured in his homeland by a warring people and sold into slavery – 'into the hands of the Christians, who bound me and sent me on board a great ship,' as Said wrote in his memoir.[15]

During his time as a slave, Said became the focus of a de facto public relations battle. Among those who publicly advocated for his conversion was Francis Scott Key, the author of America's national anthem ('Oh, say, can you see, by the dawn's early light'), who arranged for an Arabic-language Bible to be sent to Said in 1819. The slave was eventually baptized. Because of newspaper accounts and word-of-mouth that Said might have been an Arab prince before his capture, he became one of America's best-known slaves in the 1820s.

Around the same time, another Muslim slave in the American south, Abdul Rahman Ibrahima, drew attention from the wider public because he was freed from bondage after the intervention of the Moroccan government, which petitioned President John Quincy Adams for Ibrahima's release in the belief that he was a Moroccan subject. Ibrahima was not. He was originally from Timbo (in present-day Guinea), born to a prominent Muslim ruler – an *almaamy* (spiritual head) who had his son educated in military and religious ways. Ibrahima knew how to read and write Arabic, and his Arabic letter appealing for his release found its way to the Moroccan sultanate. The White House personally asked Ibrahima's Mississippi owner, Thomas Foster, to release the man he had enslaved for almost 40 years, and Foster agreed – as long as Ibrahima left the United States for Africa. Ibrahima did, but not before going to America's north and embarking on a year-long campaign to raise money to buy his children out of slavery, too. During this period, Ibrahima met at the White House with Adams, and at the office of Secretary of State Henry

Clay ('they both received me very kindly,' he wrote[16]), and succeeded in raising enough funds from abolitionists and others to eventually allow eight of his descendants freedom and passage to Liberia.

During his four decades of slavery in Natchez, Mississippi, Ibrahima lived both an Islamic life and a life of compromise. He married a non-Muslim woman, Isabella, who followed Baptist traditions and took her husband and their children to Baptist church services. Ibrahima continued to tell people he followed principles laid out in the Quran, including abstaining from alcohol, and practiced Arabic by writing words in the dirt on Foster's plantation. In Timbo, Ibrahima had grown up memorizing passages of the Muslim holy book, and also formally studied Islam in West Africa's most important religious centers, Timbuktu and Djenne. Though he told members of the American Colonization Society during his fundraising tour that he had converted to Christianity and would proselytize for their religion upon returning to Africa, when Ibrahima finally left America and landed in Liberia in 1829, he renounced those pledges. Even during his time in America, Ibrahima had been critical of the lack of religious devotion among whites who professed to be good Christians yet allowed the enslavement of others. He once told Cyrus Griffin, editor of the Natchez paper, *Southern Galaxy*, that the New Testament was a 'very good law (but) you no follow it,' and also said, 'You no pray often enough.'[17]

Still, Ibrahima played the part of would-be convert after leaving Natchez, meeting white Americans who wanted to sponsor his return to Africa and pay for his children's manumission. He'd been known for most of his slave life as 'Prince', a name given to him by Foster after an interpreter told the plantation owner that Ibrahima was the son of royalty. In a portrait that was drawn during Ibrahima's fundraising tour by a prominent painter named Henry Inman, the now-former slave is shown in a regal pose, dressed in a fine coat and white shirt with collars that jutted up around his face. Ibrahima was 66, with gray hair that sprouted from his temples. His image was printed in northern newspapers, and he was lauded by prominent officials, including Massachusetts Congressman Edward Everett, who saw Ibrahima write what they thought was the Lord's Prayer in Arabic. Instead, Ibrahima had written the *Fatiha*, the Quran's first chapter. 'When I saw him at Washington, after a long life passed in slavery,' Everett said, 'he was able to read the [Quran] with fluency, and wrote the Arabic character with great elegance.'[18]

Ibrahima's tour became a minor issue in the 1828 presidential election after Foster and a former Natchez supporter, newspaper editor Andrew Marschalk, complained that Ibrahima was violating his release terms by campaigning for his offspring's release and not going immediately to Africa. Foster and Marschalk said Adams was ultimately responsible for the legal breach, was fomenting belligerency among southern slaves, and undeserving of southern support in his bid to serve a second White House term. The controversy cemented Ibrahima's place in recorded history.

Between 1619, when slavery was introduced to the British colony of Virginia, and 1865, when the thirteenth amendment to the US Constitution officially banned slavery, tens of thousands of Muslim slaves were the property of American landowners. Some estimates place the number at 30,000;[19] other estimates suggest it was more than 100,000.[20] Whatever the actual number, these Muslims left behind narratives of their captivity in Africa, their voyages across the Middle Passage, their forced lives in America, and – if they were lucky – their escape from enslavement. One of the few known communities of Muslim slaves in antebellum America lived on Georgia's Sapelo Island, under the tutelage of Bilali Mohammed, in isolation from the rest of the contiguous south. Slaves would hear about other slaves through gossip and other channels. And there were instances of American Muslim slaves communicating with Muslims from other countries – as when a Muslim in China named Yang, encouraged by an American missionary who knew Said, sent the slave a letter in 1858 – but these were exceptional cases. The majority of American slaves lived and died in anonymity. Those like Said, who lived to a time when photography captured his image not once but twice, became the apotheosis of a slave with origins in Muslim Africa, where Islam had been planted 800 years before the advent of American slavery. In the two photos – one taken in the 1850s, when Said was in his eighties; the other taken a few years later – Said has a pensive, even angry, look on his face.

By contrast, a painting of Ayuba Suleiman Ibrahima Diallo, done by celebrated English painter William Hoare when the former slave had stopped in England on his way back to Africa, shows the former Maryland servant in traditional African robes and headdress, a look of nobility and confidence on his face. Around his neck, draped across his chest, is a Quran that hangs from a strap. The Quran appears to be in a brown leather pouch, whose color matches the color of the cloth atop Diallo's head. His hair is long, in an Afro style that comes down below his ears. When Ibrahima stepped ashore at Natchez in chains, he also had long hair, in the style that signified his membership of the elite Muslim tribe that ruled over the Futa Jallon region of West Africa. Within days, Foster would cut off Ibrahima's locks, and patronizingly called him 'Prince' – as if it were unfathomable that a man of royal heritage could emanate from a continent that many Americans considered backward and barbaric. Literate slaves like Diallo (who could write out the Quran from memory), Ibrahima, and Said were regularly called 'Moors' by white southerners who presumed they were dark-skinned Arabs, not Africans. The writings that these Muslim slaves left behind set the record straight, introducing those who read them to the intricacies and depth of their faith and history. During their enslavement in America, they were often the first Muslims that people had met. While many Americans ridiculed their practices as odd and off-putting, other Americans became fascinated with the slaves' religious behavior, even expressing admiration. In *Some Memories of the Life of Job,* Bluett describes the first time he met Diallo, who had been brought from his prison cell to meet Bluett and several other men in an establishment called 'Goaler's House', which served alcohol.

He was brought into the Tavern to us, but could not speak one Word of English. Upon our Talking and making Signs to him, he wrote a Line or two before us, and when he read it, pronounced the Words Allah and Mahommed; by which, and his refusing a Glass of Wine we offered him, we perceived he was a Mahometan, but could not imagine of what Country he was, or how he got thither; for by his affable Carriage, and the easy Composure of his Countenance, we could perceive he was no common Slave.[21]

Bluett's words crystalize Islam's place in eighteenth-century America: The religion wasn't called 'Islam' but 'Mahometanism'. This widespread misrepresentation would continue for another century. By then, descendants of Muslim slaves who practiced the religion of their forefathers were virtually non-existent. In their place were white Americans who adopted the religion of Islam, new Muslim immigrants from the Middle East, and a new generation of African-Americans who believed that Islam was their true faith, even though the religion they practiced was markedly different from the religion that Diallo, Said, and Ibrahima had brought with them on their forced journey across the waters of the Atlantic Ocean.

2 'White Muslims' Change the Face of a Faith

American Islam, 1890–1910

In the Union Square area of New York City, on a crisp December morning in 1893 when the temperature hovered around 40 degrees Fahrenheit, a group of men made their way to the third floor of a prominent bank building. John Lant, Emin Nabakoff, Alexander Russell Webb, and their cohorts all identified as Muslims, and all of them wanted to make history. Never before in America's most prominent city had a muezzin shouted the *adhan* (call to prayer) in public for everyone to hear – until Lant poked his head out a third-floor window of the Union Square bank building on 10 December, and chanted in Arabic, '*Allahu Akbar; Ash-had an la ilaha illa llah*' ('God is greater than any description. I testify there is no deity except for God'). Lant's voice echoed across Union Square's sidewalks at 11 a.m., and when he was done, Nabakoff, Webb, and the others knelt down in an adjacent room and prayed toward Mecca. The next day, the *New York Times* splashed the news on its front page ('New-York's First Muezzin Call: Mr. Lant Uses a Third-Story Window for a Minaret')[1] and gave readers a detailed description of the event, noting that Lant was dressed in Islamic robes, and that the adhan segued into a meeting of the Society for the Study of Islam, where Nabakoff was the principal speaker and talked on the subject of 'Islam in America'.

What was not pointed out that day was that Lant, Nabakoff, and Webb were white. The trio's embrace of Islam (or the 'Mohammedan' faith, as the 11 December 1893 *New York Times* described it) was a major turning point in the history of American Islam. Never before had whites in America so boldly proclaimed their allegiance to the religion – a religion that, since the founding of the nation, had often been vilified as an enemy of Christianity, as the faith of Ottoman despots and Barbary Coast corsairs, as the antithesis of American values. In the 1700s and early 1800s, when hundreds of US seamen and soldiers were captured in Mediterranean waters by North African regimes, those who 'turned Turk' or 'turned Moor' – i.e. converted to Islam – during their captivity were deemed traitors to America. In 1703, Puritan minister Cotton Mather proclaimed Muslims to be 'filthy disciples of Mahomet' during a sermon about American captives in North Africa.[2] Noting that some white American prisoners had converted to Islam during their imprisonment abroad, Mather called them 'wretched' Christians, labeled the Quran as 'accursed' and called the Muslim Prophet Muhammad an 'impostor'.[3]

In the nineteenth century, one of the first white Americans to convert to Islam was Lewis Heximer, a US soldier on the USS *Philadelplhia*, which was captured by forces of the Algerian Dey in 1803, in the waters off Tripoli. Heximer converted during his captivity over the next two years, giving himself the new name of Hamet Amerikan. Like Thomas Smith, another American captive in Tripoli who renounced Christianity, Heximer began dressing like his captors – prompting another captive to write in his diary, 'These men had all been circumcised and now wore the turban.'[4]

This was conversion by coercion, in a foreign land under conditions similar to those faced by West African slaves in America. The public testament in New York by Lant, Nabakoff, and the turban-wearing Webb – coinciding with Webb's campaign to spread the message of Islam and educate, if not convert, other white Americans – marked a dramatic new phase in Islam's development in America. Webb's mission was being funded by wealthy Muslims from India whom Webb had met after resigning his position as American consul in the Philippines. He had plans to build America's first mosque and was already publishing America's first Muslim-oriented newspaper, the *Moslem World*, whose front page was adorned with an image of a mosque with minarets, below which was the motto, 'To Spread the Light of Islam in America'.

Webb described himself as a 'missionary'[5] who was going to introduce Americans to 'practical' Islam – an Islam that he said was 'a sensible, pure, everyday religion which we [he and other US followers] believe to be far superior to Christianity, and we shall seek in every way to supplant Christianity with it [...] Eventually we expect to erect mosques in all the leading cities.'[6] Webb also imagined a day when an English-language copy of the Quran was 'in each house in the United States'.[7]

Despite Webb's enthusiasm in 1893, his organization built no mosques, distributed relatively few Qurans, and presented little evidence that it converted anyone to Islam. Still, Webb succeeded in raising Islam's profile in the United States. Through speeches, parlor talks (his preferred forum), meetings, publications, and journalistic articles, Webb convinced influential newspapers and scores of Americans that Islam was an important religion worthy of further study. In commenting on Webb's effort to reframe Americans' understanding of Islam, the *New York Mercury* opined, 'We must get into something that we can believe in, at least until we find it fallacious.'[8]

This new openness to Islam – however limited – paralleled an influx of Muslim immigration to America between 1865 and 1910. Hailing mainly from the remnants of the Ottoman Empire in Eastern Europe and the Middle East, these immigrants – numbering around 40,000[9] – were from greater Syria, Turkey, Yemen, India, Poland, Albania, and other countries. They spoke different languages, and adhered to different schools of Islam, but they all had three things in common: they arrived in America seeking economic opportunities; they lived in scattered regions of the country, essentially comprising different entities of American Islam; and they were all subjected to differing racial classifications, at times labeled by themselves and others as 'white' or 'Caucasian', at other times labeled as distinctly non-white.

The white/non-white distinction was crucial, since it helped determine whether they received legal naturalization – or even entry into America. Social status was also at stake. US immigration policy favored people who were considered Caucasian. In 1910, the United States Immigration Commission, headed by senators and members of Congress, issued a major report that sought to distinguish between Arab Christians and Arab Muslims, and between Indian Hindus and Indian Muslims. The report concluded that the designation 'white race' or 'Caucasian' was also synonymous with 'Caucasic', 'European', and 'Eurafrican'[10] – which meant that even races that were 'dark in color or aberrant in other directions'[11] may thus be categorized as Caucasian. Included in this group, said the commission, were: 'The dark Hindus and other peoples of India [...] because of their possessing an Aryan speech.'[12] The designation excluded Indian Muslims, although their language (Urdu) is a kind of linguistic mirror to Hindi. The same report said that Aramaic-speaking Syrians, even those with 'Arabian blood' and those who spoke Arabic, 'belong to the Semitic branch of the Caucasian race'. Arab Muslims did not.[13]

Webb, who was then known as Muhammed Webb or Muhammed Alexander Russell Webb, promulgated race and class differences among Muslims, telling the *New York Times* in February 1893 that he would avoid working with non-white Muslims. 'There are a few Mussulmans [Muslims] in New York,' wrote the *Times,* 'but they are mostly peddlers and low-caste Hindus ['Hindus' being the name for anyone from India], and Muhammed Webb will not associate himself with them.'[14]

Faced with this kind of social environment, some Muslim immigrants changed their names to Christian ones and passed as de facto white non-Muslims. (In a 2007 poll of Muslim-Americans released by the Pew Research Center, 64 percent of respondents from the Arab region identified themselves as 'white'.[15]) Despite the social pressures, new Muslim immigrants in the late nineteenth century were welcomed – if not with open arms then with a reluctant acceptance – as people who could help transform the industrial and agricultural belts of post-Civil War America. The country had expanded westward, and it needed people willing to do hard work not just in the new territories but in established ones. In the Midwestern state of North Dakota, Muslim families from greater Syria arrived in the early 1900s to work as farmers and homesteaders; they were rewarded by the US government with free parcels of land in return for cultivating the property. In southern Maine, Albanian and Turkish Muslims were employed to work in textile mills. In the New York borough of Brooklyn, Tatar Muslims – descendants of Turkic-speaking people from Central Asia and Europe – came from Poland, Lithuania, and Russia and established the American Mohammedan Society in 1907. Around the same time in Chicago, 'Bosniacs' – Muslims from Bosnia, which had been part of the Ottoman Empire from the fifteenth to nineteenth centuries – began Dzemijetul Hajrije (the Benevolent Society) of Illinois as a cultural and financial mainstay for local Muslims. And in Michigan City, Indiana, merchants and peddlers from greater Syria found refuge and a place to do business. Mosques (some of America's first) would eventually follow.

Foreshadowing this immigration, in 1856 the US military recruited a Muslim Ottoman subject from greater Syria, Hajji Ali, to be a lead rider in its experimental camel corps. The camels, like Ali, were taken from the Middle East to the southwestern United States, which was new territory – with deserts, mountains, and other hard-to-navigate terrain – that the military wanted to explore more efficiently. Ali's first name was an honorific given to him for completing the *hajj* to Mecca, but his US recruiters resorted to calling him a reductive version of his real name: 'Hi Jolly'. After the camel experiment ended in failure, Ali remained in the United States, changing his name to Philip Tedro, and marrying a non-Muslim woman, Gertrudis Serna, in 1880.

The first Muslim immigrants to America often intermarried with non-Muslims, or their offspring intermarried or de-emphasized Islam. In 1902, Mary Juma and her husband Hassin – from greater Syria – settled in North Dakota, and the next year had a son Charles, who as a adult attended Lutheran Church services. In 1908, Mohammed Asa Abu-Howah was naturalized as a US citizen under his Christianized American name, A. Joseph Howar, which he adopted on the ship to his new homeland. Abu-Howah was born near Jerusalem, living in the Holy Land till around the age of 20. 'People I met on the boat told me I'd better change my name,' Howah relayed to a journalist in 1975, seven years before his death. 'They said it labeled me as a Muslim, and no immigration officer would allow a Muslim to enter the United States.'[16]

Immigration couldn't do anything, though, about people already living in the United States who wanted to connect to Islam. Webb's whiteness and his prominence – he had been a journalist before taking his position as consul in Manila – gave him advantages that Howah and other immigrant Muslims could never obtain. Webb had a national and even international platform, and he used his celebrity whenever possible to stress that Islam was compatible with other religions, including Christianity. Webb himself was a practicing Theosophist – a person who believed that all faiths were guides for people to seek higher truths – and he proclaimed that basic tenets of Islam and Theosophy (especially the emphasis that both placed on inner truth) could be conjoined.

With his long beard, robes, and wearing a turban or fez, Webb was an object of curiosity wherever he went. For many Americans at the turn of the nineteenth century, Webb *was* the face of Islam. At the 1893 World's Parliament of Religions, held in Chicago at the World Columbian Exposition, Webb represented not just American Islam but global Islam, and proclaimed in an address to attendees, 'There is not a (Muslim) on earth who does not believe that ultimately Islam will be the universal faith [...] I have faith in the American intellect, in the American intelligence, and in the American love of fair play, and will defy any intelligent man to understand Islam and not love it.'[17] Webb also tried to defend Islam from an association with polygamy, saying the religion's allowance of multiple wives was misunderstood in the West as a big sign of Islam's aberrance when it was really little practiced in Islam. 'There are', Webb said, 'thousands and thousands of people who seem to be in mortal terror that the curse of polygamy is to be inflicted upon them at once.'[18]

Webb was referring to the 1891 Immigration Act that banned polygamists from entering the United States. Ostensibly, the legislation was aimed at Mormons who immigrated to America to settle in the state of Utah, but the law was also used to target Muslims. (The Act was another reason that many Muslims in

America – or those attempting to get in – played down their religious affiliation.) Webb also used his time at the podium to question what was then one of America's most popular reference works on Islam: Washington Irving's two-volume work, *Mahomet and his Successors*, first published in 1849 and subsequently republished in various editions. The books, by the pre-eminent American writer (his best-known short story: *The Legend of Sleepy Hollow*), portrayed the Prophet Muhammad as a sex-starved narcissist who also had his positive traits.

What Webb didn't note in Chicago was that Irving's books – like the publications of Webb himself – helped establish a dialogue on Islam at a time in America when the country had very few Muslims. So even though Islam had yet to a make a significant foothold in the United States, the religion was still a topic of discussion and interest – at least among white American intellectuals, newspaper editorialists, and others who (like Irving and Webb himself) had traveled abroad and had met Muslims or come into direct acquaintance with their culture. Ralph Waldo Emerson was one such person. A Harvard-trained Unitarian minister, Emerson was, in the mid 1800s, America's most prominent essayist and thinker – a man who introduced Muslim Persian poets to US audiences, and who, in an 1860 essay called 'Worship', implied that Islam had a role to play in the coming decades. Emerson wrote:

> The religion which is to guide and fulfill the present and coming ages, whatever else it be, must be intellectual. The scientific mind must have a faith which is science. 'There are two things,' said Mahomet, 'which I abhor, the learned in his infidelities, and the fool in his devotions.' Our times are impatient of both, and specially of the last. Let us have nothing now which is not its own evidence.[19]

Webb, Lant, and others found that evidence in Islam, embracing it with more fervor than many of the immigrant Muslims who made it to the burgeoning United States. The *New York Times* would devote scores of articles to Webb's efforts to proselytize, and months before the muezzin call in New York, the paper featured Webb in stories that described his Islamic transformation. On 11 December 1893, though, the muezzin call – albeit on the front page – received just four paragraphs, and shared space with other attention-grabbing headlines, such as: 'Hurled him from the Car: An Express Messenger Defends his Charge from a Robber' and 'Paradise for Tramps: Great Immigration into Kansas, Thanks to Gov. Lewelling'. America had more on its mind than the actions of a small group of white Muslims. In retrospect, though, the muezzin call in Union Square was the first serious public foothold of Islam in America.

No longer was Islam at the margins, reduced to a subject in the academy, or articles about foreign wars, or practiced by people – immigrants and others – who lived anonymous lives. This was Islam embodied by the nineteenth-century equivalent of 'native Americans' – white people like Webb who were born and raised in the United States and who reached a status of success that was the envy of others. This was Islam that went to the historic center of America's biggest city and revealed itself not in English but in the original language of the Prophet Muhammad. For that one morning in 1893, Webb helped turn the bank building, located at 8 Union Square, into a de facto mosque whose members – however small in number – embodied an important new chapter in American Islam.

3 Islam Becomes a Religion of the Nation

American Islam, 1920–1965

In the mid 1930s, amidst America's Great Depression, a million-copy bestseller, *The Passing of the Great Race*, was published in its fourth edition. The book by Madison Grant, a US eugenicist, sought to explain the 'inferiority'[1] of non-Nordic races. Among those judged to be 'subordinate'[2] – and worthy of segregation, if not sterilization and killing – were black Americans and 'the hyphenated aliens in our midst upon whom we have carelessly urged citizenship'.[3] Arabs, the tome said, were descendants of a people who specialized in stealing and killing. A diatribe against immigrant groups and African-Americans, *The Passing of the Great Race* typified the extreme level of prejudice that existed in the early part of the twentieth century, when US cities – even those in the 'liberal' north – were divided along lines of race and ethnicity. Detroit was typical. 'Negro districts' were separate from white neighborhoods, and in surrounding areas immigrant groups that worked the automobile factories lived on blocks in their own separate ethnic groups. A growing number of Muslims resided in the Detroit area in the 1930s, including Wallace Fard

Muhammad and Hussein Karoub, who responded to the social conditions they faced in very different ways.

Muhammad advocated that African-Americans embrace Islam as their 'original' religion, saying they were descendants from Mecca in Saudi Arabia – from a tribe called 'Shabazz' that white Europeans had enslaved in the mid 1500s – and that Africans had fallen from their origins as earth's 'noblest' people. It was not white Christians who were superior, said Muhammad, but black Muslims – and Islam, he said, would return Christian-oriented African-Americans to their rightful place in the world. Muhammad, who claimed to be from Mecca himself and was said to be the son of an African father and white mother, preached (starting in 1930) to Detroit's black community for three years, leading to the establishment of the Nation of Islam and its first mosque, located on Hastings Street in Detroit's 'Black Bottom' district. Thousands of poor blacks joined the Nation of Islam, with Muhammad revered as a prophet sent by God to deliver his message of salvation and racial separateness from 'blue-eyed devils'.

Meanwhile, Karoub – a Sunni imam from greater Syria – was reaching out to Muslims of all backgrounds and races from his home in Highland Park, the Detroit suburb where the Ford Motor Company had established a state-of-the-art automobile factory. Karoub had immigrated to America in 1912, following his brother, Muhammad Karoub, who had forged a successful career as a real estate developer. The brothers had already established a house of worship in 1921, the Moslem Mosque of Highland Park (one of America's first fully fledged mosques), but it had closed, and Hussein Karoub, who had worked on Ford's assembly lines, was spending his time teaching Arabic to area residents and performing religious functions that the community needed. In 1938, efforts to re-establish a mosque were realized with the founding of the American Moslem Society in Dearborn, the Detroit suburb where the Ford Motor Company had built another automobile plant. One of the society's main goals – supported by Hussein Karoub – was to 'teach all Moslems, irrespective of sect, the doctrines of Islam'.[4] Even non-practicing Muslims were welcome at the mosque, whose atmosphere was as much that of a community hall as a strict religious institution.

The 1930s and early 1940s were a time of transition for American Muslims, and Detroit was an epicenter for the conflicting movements that were creating startling changes from coast to coast. Detroit had become a magnet for people seeking jobs and a better life. Karoub and other Arab and Muslim immigrants had arrived in the early part of the century to work in the burgeoning auto industry, which recruited workers from the Middle East. Blacks from the American south had also moved in great numbers to Detroit, drawn by employment in the auto industry and its corollary economies. Door to door, Wallace Fard Muhammad (who was also known as Wallace D. Fard) sold silks and clothing in the neighborhoods adjoining Detroit's plants. Muhammad's top religious disciple, Elijah Poole (who later changed his last name to Muhammad), labored for six years in Chevrolet's Detroit plant before losing his job in the Great Depression. The opening of mosques was evidence that these communities of new residents wanted to establish roots in the Detroit area. When the Moslem Mosque of Highland Park opened in 1921, about 16,000 Muslims lived in the Detroit area.[5] Ten years later, thousands more resided there, along with several thousand blacks who had joined the Nation of Islam.

The number of Muslim immigrants would have been higher if not for a series of US anti-immigration laws in the 1920s that targeted people from Eastern Europe, the Middle East, Africa, and Asia. Alarmed at the increasing number of non-Nordic

Europeans in the United States, legislators – encouraged by President Calvin Coolidge ('America must be kept American'[6]) and eugenicists such as Madison Grant – drafted the Johnson–Reed Act of 1924, which set severe quotas on people from countries other than Germany, Great Britain, Ireland, and a smattering of other northern European nations. In the following two years, more than 50,000 Germans entered the United States while only 100 were officially allowed entry from such Muslim-majority countries as Turkey, Syria, Egypt, Palestine, and Albania.[7] Grant claimed victory in the introduction to the fourth edition of his book:

> *The Passing of the Great Race*, in its original form, was designed by the author to rouse his fellow-Americans to the overwhelming importance of race and to the folly of the 'Melting Pot' theory, even at the expense of bitter controversy. This purpose has been accomplished thoroughly, and one of the most far-reaching effects of the doctrines enunciated in this volume and in the discussions that followed its publication was the decision of the Congress of the United States to adopt discriminatory and restrictive measures against the immigration of undesirable races and peoples.[8]

Despite Grant's celebration, American Muslims in Detroit and other US cities were expanding their presence at the grass-roots level, giving Muslims (and potential Muslims) more choices on where to pray and what branch of Islam they would identify with. In the Detroit area, besides the American Moslem Society (a Sunni mosque) and the Nation of Islam's Muhammad Temple No. 1, there was Hashemite Hall, a Shiite-oriented worship space that opened in Dearborn in 1940. Nine years later, Detroit's growing Albanian-Muslim community welcomed Vehbi Ismail, an Albanian imam trained at Cairo's al-Azhar University, who established the Albanian American Moslem Society.

In Chicago, where the Nation of Islam had expanded, a Muslim sect called the Ahmadiyya, rooted in India, founded a mosque in 1921 that continued to draw many converts, especially among African-Americans. The Ahmadiyya believe that the group's founder, Mirza Ghulam Ahmad, was a prophet sent to finish the fulfillment of Islamic practice (a heretical idea among mainstream Muslims). The Ahmadiyya's first American missionary, Muhammad Sadiq, spent time in Detroit and was invited to attend the 1921 opening of the Moslem Mosque of Highland Park, where he said that Islam 'treads underfoot all racial prejudices'[9] – a social-justice theme that Sadiq would repeat over and over during his time in the United States.

In 1934 in Cedar Rapids, Iowa, area Muslims who had emigrated from greater Syria built what they considered to be the first permanent American mosque (and is today nicknamed the 'Mother Mosque of America'). People who walked up the steps in 1934 were greeted with a sign in English and Arabic that read, 'Moslem Temple' and 'al-Nadi al-Islami' (meaning 'Islamic Club'). Another mosque sprang up in Ross, North Dakota – this one also begun, in 1929, by immigrants from greater Syria (and torn down in the 1960s). In 1924 in Michigan City, Indiana, local Muslims founded a Shiite Islamic center called the Asser El Jadeed ('the new generation') Arabian Islamic Society. Around the same time, Polish-speaking Muslims established a mosque in Brooklyn, while in 1932, in Pittsburgh, Pennsylvania, African Muslims influenced by a man named Noble Drew Ali founded what they called the First Muslim Mosque.

Ali occupies an important role in the history of American Islam. A progenitor of the black-consciousness philosophy extolled later by the Nation of Islam, Ali founded the Moorish

Science Temple of America, which taught that US blacks were really 'Moors' – part of an Asiatic race descended from the people of north Africa and, before that, Moabites from the Holy Land who had founded Mecca. Ali and his cohorts wore clothing (fezzes, turbans, long robes) that signified a connection to this supposed Asiatic past. They also used a holy book called the 'Holy Koran of the Moorish Science Temple of America', which said that the North Carolina-born Ali was the world's last prophet, required people to 'obey the ordinance of Allah', and stressed that 'the fallen sons and daughters of the Asiatic Nation of North America need to learn to love instead of hate.'[10] At a time in America when race relations were at a low point, and the Ku Klux Klan was gaining popularity throughout the American south and even in the north, the temple's message stood out. The Moorish Science Temple of America claimed tens of thousands of members. After Ali's death in 1929, the subsequent fighting among his followers for control of the organization – and revelations about Ali's involvement with young women – undermined the temple's credibility, and in the 1930s and 1940s it was the Nation of Islam that filled an important political and religious vacuum for many African-Americans.

In 1948, Malcolm Little, a black high-school dropout incarcerated in prison for larceny, underwent a conversion to Islam under the sway of the Nation of Islam, which taught its members to pray five times a day, abstain from alcohol and gambling, and to revere Wallace Fard Muhammad as the one whom God had sent to save his people. Members, who looked upon Elijah Muhammad as the living embodiment of Wallace Fard Muhammad's message, believed that a white scientist named Yacub had created white people from blacks seven millennia earlier, and that Armageddon was about to liberate black Americans from whites' oppression. To rid themselves of any association with white slave masters, members' last names were replaced with the letter 'X.' Upon his release from a Massachusetts prison in 1952, Malcolm Little – soon to be called Malcolm X – moved to Detroit to live with his brother Wilfred Little. Like Elijah Muhammad and Hussein Karoub, Malcolm X found his way to Detroit's auto plants for employment, and to a public embrace of his faith that put him in a position of leadership and scrutiny. Within the decade, Malcolm X would transform the Nation of Islam into a viable national organization, establishing mosques from Boston to Los Angeles and becoming a lightning rod for the version of Islam propagated by the Nation of Islam.

Was the group preaching a dangerous factionalism or a bona fide religion? Malcolm X argued the latter, insisting that the Nation of Islam was the answer for a people (African-Americans) who had not been given their full rights as citizens since the advent of slavery. The Nation of Islam, as funneled through the charismatic words of Elijah Muhammad and Malcolm X, was a powerful draw for African-Americans who were essentially outcasts in their own country. W.E.B. Du Bois wrote profoundly about the 'double consciousness' of African-Americans, of having 'warring souls' that are divided into halves of race and nationality. In his book, *Black Pilgrimage to Islam*, Robert Dannin reflects the same idea when he talks about the 'double minority status of African American Muslims',[11] but Dannin pinpoints a third level of consciousness that prompted tens of thousands of African-Americans to embrace Islam: poverty. Desperate to escape the crippling economic straitjacket that was suffocating large swaths of their community, African-Americans looked to Islam – a religion that had had no association with American racism or American slavery – for spiritual stability and hope that their lives would improve. The Nation of Islam gave them dignity. By 1960, the Nation

of Islam claimed 50,000 'believers',[12] while active members –
those who followed all the Nation's precepts and participated
in its meetings and religious functions – numbered as few as
5,000.[13] Regardless, millions of Americans knew about the
Nation of Islam through media reports and TV broadcasts,
with Malcolm X articulating a political/religious/activist vision
that became a benchmark for other leaders – and Muslims
– to consider and debate. In 1959, when African-American
TV journalist Louis Lomax interviewed Malcolm X,[14] Lomax
quoted the words of Elijah Muhammad, who reportedly said:
'The only people born of Allah are the black nation, of whom
the so-called American Negro are descendants.' Malcolm
X said the words were precise and true, then said that 'any
Muslim child' would identify white people with evil. For years,
the Federal Bureau of Investigation (FBI) had branded the
Nation of Islam as the 'Muslim Cult of Islam', but in 1959
Malcolm X solidified his (and the Nation of Islam's) status by
meeting in Africa and the Middle East with Muslim dignitaries
and officials. In articles and in public talks, Malcolm X said
the Nation of Islam had become 'the fastest-growing group of
Muslims in the Western Hemisphere'.[15]

Whether or not that was true, American Muslims in general
were expanding their reach beyond their local areas, trying to
establish – like the Nation of Islam – a national presence and a
connection to the greater Muslim world. Conversely, Muslim-
majority countries increasingly recognized the United States
as a nation with a growing Muslim population that could use
financial and spiritual support. These bonds were manifested
most prominently in the building of the Islamic Center of
Washington, a mosque and cultural center that opened on
Embassy Row in the nation's capital in 1957. Funded by the
governments of Saudi Arabia, Egypt, and 13 other Muslim

countries, the Islamic center catered to Washington's foreign diplomatic corps and their families, and American Muslims who lived nearby or were visiting and wanted to pray in a building inspired by the great mosques of the Arab world. The building's towering minaret, crenellated roof, external Islamic calligraphy, and other design features made it a virtual facsimile of Cairo's al-Azhar mosque and university – one of Islam's most historic institutions. In fact, the Islamic Center of Washington's first director was an al-Azhar professor, Mahmoud Hoballah, who welcomed tourists – including groups of boy scouts and women's clubs – to the center when it first opened. In August 1954, when the center was still being architecturally completed but was already operating, Hoballah told the *New York Times* that, 'Whenever a (tourist) group comes to Washington now from any part of the United States it comes to the mosque.'[16]

Americans had grown more curious about Islam. Even the president of the United States, Dwight D. Eisenhower, wanted a first-hand view of the Islamic Center of Washington, which he got in June 1957 in a visit that was notable for the emphasis he put on Islam's rightful place in the United States. Veering from his prepared remarks, Eisenhower said inside the center to a large gathering of Muslim diplomats:

> I should like to assure you, my Islamic friends, that under the American Constitution, under American tradition, and in American hearts, this Center, this place of worship, is just as welcome as could be a similar edifice of any other religion. Indeed, America would fight with her whole strength for your right to have here your own church and worship according to your own conscience. This concept is indeed a part of America, and without that concept we would be something else than what we are.[17]

Eisenhower's address – carried by TV news reports and national media – was a kind of rubber stamp, signaling Islam's formal welcoming as a 'national religion' in the United States. Eisenhower, who removed his shoes to tour the Islamic center, had been in mosques before, when military assignments had taken him to North Africa. His allusion that day to 'fighting' for the center's existence had a special significance, since he was a highly decorated hero of World War II. Eisenhower's commitment to religious pluralism, and his familiarity with Muslim traditions, undoubtedly made him sensitive to a request from a US veteran named Abdullah Igram. In 1953, Igram, the Iowa son of Lebanese immigrants, wrote to the Eisenhower administration with a request: Let Muslim American soldiers wear identity tags that announce their Islamic faith. Protestant soldiers could already order these tags – which are worn around the neck – inscribed with the letter 'P', Catholic soldiers with a 'C', and Jewish soldiers a 'J', but Muslim soldiers had no such choice, which meant their tags were stamped with 'no religion' or the space that indicated faith was left blank.

Eisenhower's administration received the letter in his first year of office, and by the time he left the White House in 1961, the Department of Defense had changed its policy and begun allowing Muslim military men to have their faith engraved on their identity tags.

'I am fighting for my right, and the right of my people, to be recognized as a religious faith,' Igram told the *Toledo (Ohio) Blade* newspaper in 1953,[18] after he had sent the letter. Igram's missive had already generated a positive reply from the Secretary of the Army, but Igram wasn't limiting himself to military matters. That year, Igram headed the International Moslem Society, a group he founded to represent Muslims in the United States and Canada. The next year, the organization morphed into the Federation of Islamic Associations, which held annual conventions and published a newsletter, the *Muslim Star*, that sought to unify North American Muslims on matters of faith and culture. The Federation of Islamic Associations was one of the first US-centered organizations to try for a broad consensus of American Muslims, and its original members – mainly from greater Syria or, like Igram, offspring of immigrants from there – were committed to working with non-Muslims. At the same time that he founded the organization, Igram also headed an effort to bring a Young Men's Christian Association to his hometown of Cedar Rapids.

By 1960, the Federation of Islamic Associations had become so recognized that its membership had reached 180,000 households, according to the organization.[19] That same year, the federation released a study that said the US Muslim population had hit 1.2 million (which would have been less than 1 percent of the 180 million people living in the United States at that time).[20] Other estimates put the US Muslim population at 200,000. Similar to the Islamic Center of Washington, elaborate mosques were being built around the United States, including Detroit, where a prominent Shia imam from Lebanon, Mohamad Jawad Chirri, had secured funding from the president of Egypt, Gamal Abdel Nasser, to buy land in the city's northwest, near Dearborn. Increasingly, foreign-born scholars were heading American organizations. The Federation of Islamic Associations would soon be led by an Egyptian academic, Mahmoud Youssef Shawarbi, who took leave from the University of Cairo to live in New York, where he advised the United Nations and also ran the Islamic Center of New York. In 1964, Shawarbi met Malcolm X, who was then based in New York. The meeting would change the course of Malcolm X's life.

The Nation of Islam had kept its distance from mainstream Muslims, but Malcolm X had decided to perform the hajj – the

Mecca pilgrimage that is one of the pillars of Islam – and he had to prove his Islamic conversion was genuine in order to obtain a visa from the Saudi Arabian consulate. The consulate had one person authorized to approve of conversions: Mahmoud Youssef Shawarbi. As it happened, Shawarbi already knew about Malcolm X through media accounts, and the two had met briefly. When they got together to go over Malcolm X's application, Shawarbi readily approved it, though not before challenging Malcolm X's views on white–black separation, and urging him to accept traditional Islam. Shawarbi gave Malcolm X a copy of *The Eternal Message of Muhammad*, a book by the Egyptian statesman Abd-al-Rahman Azzam that articulated Islam as a color-blind religion.

Malcolm X's time in Saudi Arabia coincided with his estrangement from the Nation of Islam. In December 1963, Elijah Muhammad had suspended Malcolm X from ministering for nine months, for disobeying his edict to stay silent about the assassination of President John F. Kennedy. Malcolm X had told an audience that the killing was, in effect, a result of the climate of hate that had spread unchecked around the United States – that the death was a case of the 'chickens coming home to roost'. Months earlier, Malcolm X had learned that Elijah Muhammad, who was married, had fathered several children in extra-marital affairs with two former secretaries in the Nation of Islam. The revelations shook Malcolm X's belief in Elijah Muhammad and the Nation of Islam. In Saudi Arabia, Malcolm X's assumptions about race and religion became unhinged when he met 'white-skinned' Muslims – such as Abd-al-Rahman Azzam and his son, Omar, but also strangers – who treated him with high regard. During the hajj he also saw how Muslims of all colors and ethnicities, including those with blond hair and blue eyes, paid no attention to racial differences and focused instead on their common humanity and religion. 'What I have seen and experienced on this pilgrimage has forced me to "rearrange" much of my own thought-pattern, and to toss aside some of my previous conclusions,' he wrote in a letter from Saudi Arabia to a friend in New York.[21]

Malcolm X believed that orthodox Islam could solve America's race problems. Just as he had come to see that white-complexioned Muslims could not be judged by their skin color ('it was the first time in my life that I didn't see them as "white" men'[22]), he believed that white Americans who converted to Islam – or who at least had a deep understanding of Islam's tenets – would see African-Americans without the prism of race. 'If white Americans would accept the religion of Islam,' he wrote from Saudi Arabia, 'if they would accept the Oneness of God (Allah), then they could also sincerely accept the Oneness of Man, and they would cease to measure others always in terms of their "differences in color".'[23]

Malcolm X still didn't want whites to join his new group, the Organization of Afro-American Unity, or his new religious affiliation, Muslim Mosque, Inc., but he envisioned a more integrated society where mainstream Islam – what he called 'Orthodox Islam' – had a more prominent role in America's political and social landscape. His assassination in February 1965, by followers of the Nation of Islam, cut short the life of a man whose evolving views of Islam were welcomed by other Muslims. A month before Malcolm X's death, the *New York Times* published a story on Ramadan and New York's Muslims, mentioning: Malcolm X; the Brooklyn mosque started by Polish Muslims in the 1920s; the Islamic Mission, a Brooklyn mosque co-founded by a Moroccan-born Trinidadian cleric, Daoud Ahmed Faisal, and his Bermudan-born wife, Sayeda Khadija Faisal, who led the mission's Muslim Ladies Cultural Society; the

Islamic Foundation of New York, a mosque overseen by United Nations ambassadors which had just opened on Riverside Drive but would later move to a bigger location on Third Avenue (and be renamed the Islamic Center of New York); and the International Muslim Brotherhood on 125th Street in Harlem, whose membership was primarily African-American. Immigrant Muslims, convert Muslims, and second-generation Muslims with roots in all corners of the globe were represented in these mosques.

They would soon be joined by a new wave of Muslim immigrants. In October 1965, in a changed political environment that had ended American segregation a year earlier with passage of the Civil Rights Act, President Lyndon Baines Johnson signed the Hart–Celler Act, which eliminated the immigration quotas that Madison Grant had bragged about in *The Passing of the Great Race*. No longer would people from non-Nordic countries be severely constrained from moving to the United States. President Johnson said the legislation 'corrects a cruel and enduring wrong in the conduct of the American nation'.[24] Muslims would be just one of many immigrant groups to arrive in large numbers. Their presence would change the face of American Islam yet again.

4 Islam Establishes an Identity Far Beyond the Mosque

American Islam, 1965–2010

The cold weather in America's Midwest was often on his mind, but anyone who knew Ilyas Ba-Yunus understood why. Ba-Yunus was from Karachi, the port city of Pakistan where temperatures rarely dropped below 50 degrees Fahrenheit, even in winter. In Minneapolis–Saint Paul, where he was a graduate on a Fulbright scholarship, temperatures below freezing were normal in January and February. For Ba-Yunus, the snow, wind, and chill added a memorable backdrop to his years in Minnesota, where he organized students who – like him – were Muslim and from other parts of the world. New Year's Day 1963 was of particular importance: that was when another student group in the Midwest, this one from the University of Illinois at Urbana-Champaign, approached him to form a union.

'It was a stormy and icy morning, the first day of January 1963, when change came for the Muslim American community,' Ba-Yunus recalled in 2003.[1]

The Muslim student group – at that time the Islamic Cultural Society – at the University of Minnesota had just received an invitation from the Muslim Student Association of University of Illinois at Urbana-Champaign – another of the few Muslim student groups scattered across the nation at the time – asking us to join an effort to form a national organization of Muslim students in the U.S. and Canada. It would be called 'the MSA' – Muslim Students Association. Along with 13 other local Muslim student organizations from around the country, we answered the challenge.

The challenge wasn't just logistic or financial – it was a question of commitment. Many of the student organizers only planned to be in the United States for the duration of their studies, which meant as little as a year or two. After that, they expected – as did their families – that they would return home. Their visas also required them to leave. But the Hart–Celler Act of 1965, which loosened immigration requirements, gave many students second thoughts about their plans. So did the leeway they had in America. The early to mid 1960s were a time of dramatic political change in the United States, and student groups of differing backgrounds were at the forefront of an expanding civil rights movement.

In 1962, Students for a Democratic Society – an organization headed by Tom Hayden, who would become one of America's best-known activists – held its first convention, in Michigan, and released an influential manifesto that lauded the idea of 'a participatory democracy',[2] and said its membership had moved from 'silence to activism'.[3] In 1960, the Student Nonviolent Coordinating Committee was organized in the American south to direct protests against segregationist policies that separated whites and blacks at restaurants, swimming pools, and other public spaces. The next year, students from Minnesota, Ohio, and Iowa marched in front of the White House to demonstrate against nuclear-arms testing, carrying signs that said, 'We ask you to re-evaluate U.S. nuclear policy' and 'Minnesota students fast for test ban'.[4]

For Muslim students like Ba-Yunus, student activism in the United States contrasted greatly with the political environment back home. In 1963, Pakistan was in the middle of a military dictatorship that continued through the decade amidst a war with India. In Pakistan, Ba-Yunus would have more limited prospects than if he remained in the United States. So as he worked to establish the Muslim Students Association of the United States and Canada and got his masters degree in geology from the University of Minnesota, then received a masters in sociology from Northern Illinois University, Ba-Yunus decided to stay in the Midwest and maintain his involvement in the MSA, which became the most active Muslim organization in America. The MSA's top priority – as written in 1968, in its publication called *al-Ittihad* ('The Union' or 'Unity' in English) – was to 'make Islam better understood by the Muslim students and others'.[5] Everything else was secondary, including the group's secondary goal to 'strengthen fraternal bonds among Muslim students in the U.S. and Canada'.

Composed mainly of immigrants from Pakistan, India, Iran, Saudi Arabia, Jordan, Egypt, and other countries, the Muslim Students Association invited non-students to join, and quickly expanded its mandate. In 1967, members who had graduated started an offshoot called the Islamic Medical Association of North America, followed by the Association of Muslim Scientists and Engineers in 1969, and in 1972 the Association of Muslim Social Scientists of North America. In 1966, the MSA had started an Islamic book service – a catalogue of books on Islam that it bought from publishers and resold to members. The service was advertised in *al-Ittihad* next to a section titled 'Self-Conquest', which read: 'The Holy Prophet said: "The greatest *Jehad* [holy war] is that for the conquest of self."'[6] For Ba-Yunus and other founding members of the Muslim Students Association, this conquest involved re-examining the possibilities of Islam in America.

'His master plan was to return home to Pakistan, but he realized that he had a better future in the United States, not only for himself, but for his family,' Ba-Yunus' son Asad, a Miami lawyer, tells me about his father, who died in 2007.

> He also observed that more and more Muslim immigrant students were choosing to stay, mainly because they found good-paying jobs right here in the US, and they were either getting married or having children too, and felt it was better to settle down. He too married my mother [Sayeda], who came to the US in 1969. Along the way, he realized that he had been in the US long enough to become a citizen, which in turn would allow him to sponsor family members for immigration to the US as well.

In the 1960s and 1970s, sponsoring family members was the biggest source of growth for the Muslim population. New arrivals were generally better educated than nineteenth-century Muslim immigrants, who found employment as peddlers, farmhands, laborers, and other unskilled positions (though many moved on to more advanced jobs). With graduate degrees, Ba-Yunus and other MSA members landed work in academia, business, and other white-collar professions that gave them the financial security to settle down and bring over relations and partners from their homelands. They also brought with them a conservative view of Islam. Female students weren't allowed into the Muslim

Students Association, and only observant male students – those who fasted during Ramadan and eschewed alcohol and pre-marital dating – were admitted. *Al-Ittihad* featured the writings of Sayyid Qutb, an Egyptian intellectual and Islamist who had lived in the United States in the late 1940s and criticized what he said was America's materialism, its emphasis on pop culture, its lack of religious devotion, and its treatment of blacks and other non-white people. It also featured the work of Maulana Sayyid Abul A`la Maududi, a Pakistani intellectual and Islamist who preached a rigid interpretation of Islam. Saudi Arabian funding paid for the expansion of the Muslim Students Association.[7]

Within a few years, though, the organization was influenced by its setting in the United States. Women were let in, including Sharifa Alkhateeb, whose father was Yemeni-American and whose mother was Czech-American. Alkhateeb, who was born and raised in Philadelphia, covered her hair with a hijab, the traditional Muslim headscarf, but she wore slacks and Western dresses. Women began working on *al-Ittihad*; a women's subcommittee was formed, and in 1972 Khadija Haffajee, a young educator, addressed the Muslim Students Association. Holding conventions and conferences was an idea borrowed from the Federation of Islamic Associations, the first prominent Muslim organization in America, but the Muslim Students Association distanced itself from the federation's tolerance of such activities as dancing and singing. For the founders of the Muslim Students Association, being Muslim in America meant following traditional religious norms in all public spheres. The advent of offshoot organizations like the Islamic Medical Association was a chance to bring Islamic values to the forefront of members' professions, to bring Islam out of the mosque into members' everyday lives. In 1982, the leadership of the Muslim Students Association established an organization that would be a bigger incarnation of its activist approach: the Islamic Society of North America (ISNA). No longer were students the main focus. By then, Ilyas Ba-Yunus was not just a tenured professor at the State University of New York at Cortland, he was ISNA's first president.

Today, ISNA is by far the biggest, most influential Muslim group in America. More than 300 mosques and Islamic organizations are affiliated with it, 20,000 people are members, and more than 40,000 attend its annual convention, where everything from religious instruction to matrimonial services is offered. Perhaps the biggest difference between today's ISNA and the organization that begot it in 1963 is that the majority of ISNA's members were born and raised in the United States and Canada. Instead of being immigrants, they are 'next-generation' Americans – the sons and daughters and grandchildren of immigrants – or US- and Canadian-born converts to Islam. Women compose more than a third of ISNA's membership, and in 2006 the organization elected its first female president – the first president who is also a convert: Ingrid Mattson. In 1986, Mattson converted from Christianity to Islam, after living in Paris and meeting Senegalese Muslims whose dignity and sense of religion inspired her to investigate the religion. With a PhD in Islamic Studies from the University of Chicago, Mattson became chair of the Macdonald Center for the Study of Islam and Christian–Muslim Relations at Hartford Seminary in the state of Connecticut. Her ascent to the top position of America's top Islamic organization once prompted her to ask her husband, Aamer Atek, an Egyptian engineer, 'Can you believe that I am the one who is supposed to be doing this job?'[8]

Mattson's astonishment aside, she was an ideal (hijab-wearing) face of the organization – a noticeable bookend to Ba-Yunus and other immigrant leaders who started the Muslim Students

Association and subsequent organizations. 'We're at the stage in our development as Muslims in North America where our leadership should reflect who we are as a community,'[9] Mattson said at a talk at Pennsylvania State University shortly after her election as ISNA head, a position she served for four years.

> It's natural that, by now, this organization should have someone who's a native English speaker. This is not to, in any way, belittle the contributions of all those who served ahead of me. They did a wonderful job, and built up this organization. But like every other Muslim community in the world, we should be having institutions and leadership that is home-grown and that is really embedded and relevant to the society.

The distinction between 'home-grown' and 'foreign' is one that ISNA and Muslim-Americans are highly conscious of. ISNA's critics say the organization has been overly influenced by overseas Muslims and a conservative interpretation of Islam that's incompatible with American democracy. (ISNA's – and MSA's – elaborate headquarters in Plainfield, Illinois, was financed with $21 million that the emir of Qatar helped raise.[10]) But Mattson and ISNA's new president, Mohamed Magid – who was born and raised in the Sudan – say that ISNA welcomes all varieties of Muslim faith, including Sufism, the mystical branch of Islam. In 2007, Mattson issued a strong statement of support for a new Quranic translation done by a prominent Sufi Muslim scholar in Chicago, Laleh Bakhtiar, who reinterpreted a passage that for centuries had been used by men to justify hitting their wives. The passage – verse 34 of chapter 4 – has traditionally been written to say that men can strike their wives at a certain point of disobedience. For example, the English version of the Quran translated by

Abdullah Yusuf Ali in India in 1934 – one of the world's most popular translations, and one that is widely used in the United States – translates the verse this way:

> Men are the protectors and maintainers of women, because Allah has given the one more [strength] than the other, and because they support them from their means. Therefore the righteous women are devoutly obedient, and guard in [the husband's] absence what Allah would have them guard. As to those women on whose part ye fear disloyalty and ill-conduct, admonish them [first], [next], refuse to share their beds, [and last] beat them [lightly]; but if they return to obedience, seek not against them means [of annoyance]: for Allah is Most High, Great [above you all].[11]

As translated by Bakhtiar in *The Sublime Quran*, men are told to 'go away' from their wives, not hit them. In the passages, Bakhtiar employs '(f)' to indicate words that refer specifically to women:

> Men are supporters of wives because God has given some of them an advantage over others and because they spend of their wealth. So the ones (f) who are in accord with morality are the ones (f) who are morally obligated, the ones (f) who guard the unseen of what God has kept safe. But those (f) whose resistance you fear, then admonish them (f) and abandon them (f) in their sleeping place, then go away from them (f); and if they (f) obey you, surely look not for any way against them (f); truly God is Lofty, Great.[12]

Bakhtiar's translation was condemned by ISNA's secretary general in Canada, Mohammad Ashraf, who said he was considering banning *The Sublime Quran* from being sold at ISNA's Canadian bookstore. Ashraf told the *Toronto Star* that Bakhtiar – who has expertise in classical Quranic Arabic grammar – wasn't sufficiently trained at an institution recognized by traditional Islam. Mattson's rebuke was as lengthy as it was telling:

> The Islamic Society of North America has asked ISNA Canada Secretary General to retract his statement that he would consider 'banning' Laleh Bakhtiar's translation of the meaning of the Qur'an and his questioning of Bakhtiar's authority to undertake such a translation. ISNA is an umbrella organization that strives to represent the diversity of North American Islam. ISNA has long recognized the validity of different schools of Islamic thought, theology and doctrine [...] ISNA supports and encourages honest debate and scholarship on issues affecting the Muslim community. In particular, we have long been concerned with the misuse of Islam to justify injustice towards women. ISNA held its first domestic violence conference over ten years ago, and since that time, has held numerous training and education seminars to promote domestic harmony and prevent violence against women. It should be noted, in fact, that Bakhtiar's interpretation of Qur'anic verse 4:34 is not new, although we do not deny that she arrived at her position independently. A similar interpretation was offered by Dr Abdul Hamid Abu Sulayman, Rector of the International Islamic University of Malaysia, in a 2003 special edition of 'Islamic Horizons,' ISNA's flagship publication. It is unfortunate that many Muslims are unaware of the depth and sophistication of Qur'anic exegesis.[13]

Mattson's admonition of Ashraf, endorsement of Bakhtiar's right to translate the verse, and condemnation of the 'misuse of Islam to justify injustice towards women' marked a new turning point in ISNA's – and American Islam's – evolution. In the 1970s, the exchange of views would have been considered blasphemous – the airing of 'dirty laundry' that was of little use in the public domain. ISNA's 2010 convention in Illinois highlighted other dramatic changes in the organization. While the original founders of the Muslim Students Association had castigated secular music at Islamic events, the 2010 convention featured a Swedish-Lebanese pop singer, Maher Zain, who has worked with Nadir Khayat, the Swedish-Moroccan producer famous for overseeing the music of Lady Gaga. On his Facebook page, Zain describes his genre as 'R&B, Soul and Islamic Music'. At the convention, Zain – wearing a gray suit and black shirt – sang an orchestrated tune, 'Thank You Allah', in Arabic and English, which praised God and the Prophet Muhammad, though Zain added his own youthful touches. 'Let me see some hands!'[14] Maher said on stage in the middle of the song, trying to get the audience more into the music.

ISNA's convention is usually held the same Labor Day weekend as another prominent Muslim-American convention: The Mosque Cares, the Illinois-based ministry of Warith Deen Muhammad. A son of Elijah Muhammad, who guided the Nation of Islam until his death in 1975, Warith Deen Muhammad is a seminal figure in the history of American Islam. After his father's death, Warith Deen Muhammad took over the Nation of Islam and repudiated its unorthodox views – that whites were devils created by a scientist named Yakub; that black Americans should have their own nation and were descendants of an Arabian tribe called 'Shabazz'; that Wallace Fard Muhammad, who began the Nation, was God incarnated in the flesh; and that Elijah Muhammad was a prophet. Nation followers had adhered to the message contained in Elijah Muhammad's books, including *Message to the Blackman*, which called Wallace Fard Muhammad 'our God'. Hours after his father died, Warith Deen Muhammad – who had studied Arabic and the Quran for years – addressed members of the Nation of Islam in the organization's South Side Chicago Mosque, showed them a copy of the Quran, and said: 'We have to take this down from the shelf. We say we are Muslims. What my father taught that is in this book, we will keep. What is not in this book, we have to give up.'[15]

That night, 25 February 1975, marked the end of the Nation of Islam as it had been known for 40 years. Like Malcolm X, whom he had been close to, Warith Deen Muhammad adopted orthodox (Sunni) Islam, and like Malcolm X he persuaded many of his followers to relinquish an insular view of their professed religion. Under Muhammad's urging, tens of thousands of Nation of Islam adherents, including the boxer Muhammad Ali, became mainstream Muslims. In 1976, Warith Deen Muhammad changed the name 'Nation of Islam' for 'World Community of al-Islam in the West'. (Muhammad would change the name of his organization several other times, while Louis Farrakhan – a Nation of Islam minister who'd replaced Malcolm X as Elijah Muhammad's top lieutenant – would restart the Nation of Islam.)

Despite his group's mainstream conversion, Warith Deen Muhammad – who died in 2008 – said African-American Muslims had a culture that was unique to the United States. Speaking to a British TV crew in 1981, which was filming a fashion show that featured African-American Muslim women wearing fashionable dresses and hijabs, but also dancing, Warith Deen Muhammad said:

> I wouldn't like to see us sound like Turkish people or sound like Pakistani people, with our culture, with our music, etc. – that's phony, that's imitative, that's copying somebody. You're not

yourself, and that won't help us at all. I would like to see us right where we are, take the best of what we have, and just express it as Muslims. And it will come out beautifully, and it will be our identity and culture.[16]

This choosing of identity and culture – of being able to blend personal touches with a religion that was founded in the Arabian Peninsula – is where Warith Deen Muhammad would have found common ground with Ilyas Ba-Yunus, who said the freedom to choose is what made American Islam so powerful and distinct. 'This is a society in which Muslim women observe modesty [a hijab] out of their own free will,' he wrote in 2006.[17] 'In the United States, Muslims live in a society in which they are allowed to march in protest in front of the White House.'

Undoubtedly, Ba-Yunus was alluding to the protests that paralleled the founding of the Muslim Students Association, but in the last 50 years Muslims have frequently entered the White House as advisors to presidents, Cabinet members, and invited guests. In 2010, the list of invitees to President Barack Obama's Iftar dinner – the meal to break the daily fast of Ramadan – offered a striking panorama of the breadth of American Muslims and the organizations they belong to. Besides Mattson and Magid, those invited included Anila Ali of California, a board director of the Council of Pakistan American Affairs, which was founded in 1996; Salam al-Marayati, executive director of the Muslim Public Affairs Council, a civil rights organization started in 1988; Ibrahim Vajzovic, director of the United Bosnian Association, a St. Louis (Missouri) non-profit organization that began in 2004; Hassan Jaber, head of Dearborn Michigan's Arab Community Center for Economic and Social Services, one of the largest and oldest (1971) non-profit human services organization in the United States; Nadia

Roumani, co-founder of the American Muslim Civic Leadership Institute, which began in 2006 and is centered at the University of Southern California; Ranae Quraishi, a Californian teacher who co-directs the Muslim Public Service Network, which – starting in 1994 – began placing Muslim graduates in high-profile internship positions; and Sara Najjar Wilson, a lawyer who directs the Arab American Anti-Discrimination Committee, which was founded in 1980.

Ilyas Ba-Yunus once said that ISNA represented the 'Islamic mainstream in the United States',[18] but the organization no longer has a monopoly on that. Ba-Yunus also once proclaimed – in an effort to distinguish ISNA from the Federation of Islamic Associations – that the organization 'deliberately promotes among its members as well as its affiliates, an ideological approach to Islam as a *deen* or a total system of life not to be confined to the mosque or formal daily prayers only'.[19] This description can also be applied to the myriad other Muslim organizations that have emerged alongside ISNA in the past 50 years, when new immigration, new conversions, and new births boosted America's Muslim population into the millions – perhaps as high as 9 million.

The plethora of Muslim organizations reaches into every aspect of American society – political, cultural, economic, educational. New immigrants, like Ilyas Ba-Yunus in 1963, relish the opportunities they do not have in their home countries. Ba-Yunus' son Asad says the children of Muslim immigrants also do not take for granted their activist roles. 'Throughout his life,' says Asad of his father, 'he reminded me and others that he (and we) had been given an amazing opportunity by God to live, worship, and practice our religion and celebrate our culture freely in this country, and that we should not squander it.'

They haven't. But conflicting goals and cross-purposes have divided Muslim-Americans, and many say that their faith is still not accepted as a bona fide 'American' religion. Soon after taking over the Nation of Islam from his father, Warith Deen Muhammad carried a US flag with him onstage, to symbolize his patriotism and to counterbalance his father's anti-US rhetoric. 'We should love America passionately now that America has changed so drastically within a relatively short period of time,' Warith Deen Muhammad said in 1994.[20] On Ilyas Ba-Yunus' birthday in December 2006, when he was struggling with cancer, a US flag was flown in Washington, DC, at the request of a congressman who'd been contacted by Ba-Yunus' friends and family. Asad Ba-Yunus keeps the flag in a bookcase at his home in Florida. A certificate with the flag says:

> This flag was flown for Ilyas Ba-Yunus, Ph.D, to honor your 35 years of distinguished service as a professor of sociology at the State University of New York at Cortland and as a pioneer for the American Muslim community. We the people of Central New York thank you for your dedication and commitment to educating our children, promoting diversity, understanding and tolerance, and reinforcing American values in our society.

Ilyas Ba-Yunus died in October 2007. Three years later, close to New Year's Day, Asad and his wife had their first son. He was given the name Ilyas, named after the grandfather who had come on his own to America and part of whose legacy was the next generation of American Islam. That generation has been called everything from 'patriotic' to 'radical' – classifications that were put to the test when Muslims outside the United States martyred themselves in American airspace, on a September morning when the weather was clear and the skies were full of deep, deep blue.

5 The Shock of 9/11

Crisis and Confidence for Muslim Americans

From the plateaus of Fremont, California, you can see across the bay to Palo Alto, Sunnyvale, and other cities that compose Silicon Valley, the birthplace and headquarters for Apple, Google, Facebook, and other technology companies that have revolutionized the way the world works, socializes, and does business. Since the 1980s, Silicon Valley has been a marquee name and destination for millions of visitors to the San Francisco Bay area, but for most people, Fremont was an afterthought if it even registered at all on their geographic and cultural radar – 9/11 changed that. Suddenly, after the media flocked to the city of 200,000 – after *The Economist*, the *New York Times*, the BBC, and other outlets reported that Fremont was nicknamed 'Little Kabul' – people everywhere knew that Fremont was the de facto capital of America's Afghan community. Before 9/11, Afghans were virtually invisible in mainstream America. After 9/11, they were put under a spotlight – just like Islam itself.

The history of American Islam can be divided into any number of time periods and immigration waves and evolutions, but the most dramatic turning point – one that changed the perception and very identity of American Islam more radically than any other turning point – was that Tuesday morning in late summer when 19 Muslims from al-Qaeda carried out the attacks that brought down the World Trade Center towers in New York, severely damaged the Pentagon in Washington, DC, and killed almost 3,000 people. The hijackers and their overseers, including Osama bin Laden, could never have foreseen their impact on American Islam, but impact they had, which was four-fold:

1. A political reawakening. Prompted by a backlash against American Muslims, and widespread perceptions that Islam promoted hatred and violence, American Muslims organized to counterbalance these views and support leaders who would represent them at the local, state, and national political level. Scores of candidates ascended to office, including the first Muslim to be elected to Congress: Keith Ellison, in 2007.

2. Interfaith and curriculum outreach. Muslim groups made a more deliberate effort to engage in interfaith programs with Christian and Jewish groups, and to reach out to non-Muslim audiences in schools, universities, and other curriculum venues and forums. Before his election as president of the Islamic Society of North America in 2010, Imam Mohamed Magid spent years on interfaith programs, including one started in the days after 9/11: the Buxton Initiative, which has partnered Magid with such people as Rabbi Esther Lederman, an American woman who formerly worked on an Israeli kibbutz.

3. Media. By their own resolve and the encouragement
   of Muslim organizations, 'average' Muslims – grocers,
   business people, teachers, grandmothers, and others –
   opened their doors and were willing to be interviewed
   by media organizations, to give an alternative picture of
   American Islam and to express their views about their
   religion, their former homelands, or their current one.

4. Conversions to Islam. The post-9/11 attention on Islam
   led not just to a backlash against American Muslims but
   to an embrace of Islam by people – often students – who
   initially were curious about the religion and then decided
   to adopt it as their own. According to estimates by the
   Council on American-Islamic Relations, thousands of
   Americans since 9/11 have pledged the *shahada* – the
   profession of faith that: 'There is no god but Allah, and
   Muhammad is his messenger.'

Pre-9/11, American Islam existed in a kind of vacuum:
Muslims tended to lead insular lives – whether it was living with
or socializing with other Muslims in a community, or being
integrated into non-Muslim communities where their religious
identity wasn't an issue. The 9/11 attacks forced American
Muslims into a period of introspection and a realization that
their faith was being defined by a horrific event – and its
aftermath (including the war in Afghanistan) – that they had
no control over. American Muslims were both pushed into the
public sphere after 9/11 and volunteered themselves for the role.
Either way, there was no looking back.

'Before 9/11, the community was generally very insular,' Imam
Zaid Shakir, a prominent scholar and co-founder of Zaytuna
College, America's first Muslim liberal arts college, tells me.

What 9/11 did was, No. 1, the backlash that ensued and the growing trend of what's been described as Islamophobia – I don't like that word personally – made it clear to the community that it could no longer afford to be isolated. That isolation was contributing to the ignorance that existed in the wider society about Islam, and in that void, there were people stepping forward – so-called Islamophobes, and certain Muslim groups – defining Muslims, defining Islam, in ways that were antithetical and totally inaccurate to the interest of the community. That situation led to [other] Muslims seeing the imperative nature of stepping up and forth, defining who we are for ourselves.

Shakir was one of those who stepped up. Named in 2009 as one of the world's 500 most influential Muslims by an annual book published by Jordan's Royal Islamic Strategic Studies Centre, Shakir spoke out whenever he could – to the media, to universities, to Muslim conferences. His message of moderate Islam, his engaging speaking style, and his personal story – an African-American convert from a poor background who spent almost a decade in the Arab world studying Islam and Arabic before becoming a successful scholar – resonated with multiple audiences. But Shakir, who lives in the San Francisco Bay area, also met skeptics who questioned the intentions of American Muslims and his own religious views. Some critics claimed Shakir wanted to replace American democracy with sharia – Muslim laws handed down from the days of the Prophet Muhammad – based on comments he gave to the *New York Times* in 2006. The article, 'U.S. Muslim Clerics Seek a Moderate Middle Ground',[1] focused on Shakir and Zaytuna co-founder Sheikh Hamza Yusuf, and ended with these two paragraphs about Shakir:

He said he still hoped that one day the United States would be a Muslim country ruled by Islamic law, 'not by violent means, but by persuasion.'

'Every Muslim who is honest would say, I would like to see America become a Muslim country,' he said. 'I think it would help people, and if I didn't believe that, I wouldn't be a Muslim. Because Islam helped me as a person, and it's helped a lot of people in my community.'

Shakir's comments stoked controversy. The author Mark Steyn, in his 2006 book about the spread of Islam, *America Alone: The End of the World as we Know it*, says Shakir and other Muslim moderates secretly want to subjugate non-Muslim Americans.[2] Not true, says Shakir, who told me that the *New York Times* left out other comments that contextualized the ones left in.

'I said strictly as a religious person whose religion is Islam, I would like to see everyone be a Muslim,' he says.

But I respect the right of people to be whatever they want. And I mentioned [to the *New York Times* reporter] that I'm sure most honest Christians – because Christianity is a proselytizing religion – would like to see everyone be Christian. But that's just a personal religious statement. It's not a statement of political import that Islam should be imposed, or that it should be the state religion, or anything of the sort. Just as a Muslim, and Islam being a proselytizing religion, and having personally benefited from Islam – and I think that was the case with Malcolm X – I believe that if others became Muslim, they could benefit in particular ways. That's the context of that particular statement [to the *New York Times*].

Because of 9/11 and its lingering aftermath, American Muslims feel they have to clarify everything they say, as if they're constantly under suspicion – which they are, according to national surveys. In January 2010, for example, the Gallup Center for Muslim Studies released a survey that said Islam was, by far, the most distrusted religion in America.[3] According to the poll, 43 percent of Americans admitted they were at least 'a little' prejudiced against Muslims, with 9 percent saying they felt 'a great deal' of animosity toward Muslims. Christians were second on the list, with 18 percent of Americans admitting at least some dislike of the religious group and 4 percent expressing 'a great deal' of dislike. Jews were third, with 15 percent of respondents saying they were 'a little' prejudiced against them, and 1 percent admitting 'a great deal' of animosity. Americans who personally knew Muslims were less likely to be prejudiced against Muslims, the poll revealed. However, Americans tended to form opinions about Muslims and Islam based on little information; according to the survey, 40 percent of Americans have 'very little knowledge' of Islam, while 23 percent say they have 'none at all'. Americans' opinions, Gallup's poll suggests, are often formed by media reports of terrorist attacks and attempts, which become conflated with Islam and, by default, American Muslims.

Days before I spoke with Imam Shakir, a Muslim-American teenager was charged with plotting to explode a bomb at a Christmas tree lighting ceremony in Portland, Oregon. Mohamed Osman Mohamud, who was born in Somalia but moved to the United States as a young boy, wanted to kill as many people as possible in what would have essentially been a mini-9/11. Unbeknownst to Mohamud, the FBI had been tracking him for months and befriended him, pretending to be his accomplice. Mohamud's arrest and the attendant publicity offered a microcosm of the way American Muslims have been treated in the aftermath of 9/11. Two days after his arrest, an arsonist set fire to the mosque in Corvallis, Oregon that Mohamud had regularly visited as a student at Oregon State University. The Salman al-Farisi Islamic Center suffered damage to a business office and the burning of numerous books, prompting its imam, Yosof Wanly, to say, 'We know how it is, we know some people due to ignorance are going to perceive of these things and hold most Muslims accountable. We do what we can, but it's a tough situation.'[4] Days later, though, Wanly was thanking the community as hundreds of Corvallis residents – including Christians and Jews – organized a rally of support for the mosque and donated money and equipment to repair the building.

These two sides of America for Muslims – on the one hand, suspicion and prejudice; on the other hand, a figurative embrace – are a daily dichotomy that gets accentuated whenever an event occurs to reignite memories of 9/11. In the decade since the 2001 attacks, terrorist incidents and religious controversies have been catalysts for this double-edged reaction to Islam in America. The most heated controversy occurred in 2010, over the effort to build a Muslim center in New York two blocks from the site of the World Trade Center towers that were brought down on 9/11. Plans for the Park51 center called for a mosque, along with a 500-seat auditorium, fitness center, Olympic-size pool, culinary academy, and other facilities, fronted at street level by a façade incorporating Islamic star patterns. Park51 supporters said the mosque and its facilities were needed in Lower Manhattan, a dense area of office buildings where two older mosques – minuscule in size – serve a large population of Muslim workers who come from across metropolitan New York. Because Park51's cultural facilities would be open to people of all faiths and modeled on the inclusive approach of New York's Jewish Community Center, the building would be, organizers said, an appropriate symbol of Muslim integration 'into the fabric of the United States'.[5] Critics called the Park51 center an insensitive addition to a neighborhood that was defined by the 9/11 attacks. They argued that the building – which was hit by plane debris seconds after the 2001 tragedy – should be prevented from becoming a place of faith for a religion the hijackers professed to follow.

In public forums and in media debates, religious leaders, activists, politicians, and academics argued for and against the proposed building in a bitter national conversation that drew in people such as President Barack Obama, who threw his support behind Park51; the 2008 Republican vice presidential nominee, Sarah Palin, who said the building would be offensive to the memory of the Americans who died on 9/11 ('Peaceful Muslims, pls refudiate' she famously tweeted[6]); and 9/11 families whose relations died in the buildings, among them Todd Ouida, whose father, Herb, expressed support for Park51, saying, 'What we are doing [when we oppose the community center] is we are saying to the world that we are at war with Islam. And we can't be. I want my grandchildren to live in a better world.'[7]

Still, opposition to and reservations about the building came from key Muslim figures in the United States, including Akbar Ahmed, the Ibn Khaldun Chair of Islamic Studies at American University in Washington, DC, who told the cable network CNN that,

> I don't think the Muslim leadership has fully appreciated the impact of 9/11 on America. They assume Americans have forgotten 9/11 and even, in a profound way, forgiven 9/11, and that has not happened. The wounds remain largely open. And when wounds are raw, an episode like constructing a house of worship – even one protected by the Constitution, protected by law – becomes like salt in the wounds.[8]

Actually, those wounds are felt by both Muslim and non-Muslim Americans, according to national surveys, but for American Muslims, the wounds are complicated from a 'guilt by association' phenomenon. In a 2007 poll of Muslim-Americans released by the Pew Research Center, 53 percent said their lives were more difficult in the years after 9/11,[9] and a third of those polled said that, because of their religion, they had been verbally assaulted, physically threatened, or viewed with suspicion in the previous year.[10] The biggest problem facing US Muslims, respondents said, was 'discrimination/racism/prejudice', followed by 'being viewed as terrorists', 'ignorance about Islam', 'stereotyping', and 'negative media portrayals'.[11] (The poll found a tiny percentage of American Muslims, 1 percent, who said that suicide bombings against civilians are 'often' justified to 'defend Islam', while 8 percent said such bombings are 'sometimes' justified. Among respondents, 68 percent had an unfavorable view of al-Qaeda.[12]) American Muslims have implemented numerous public campaigns to show that their religion is a peaceful one. Several video campaigns have used an outlet that embodies the new wave of social media: YouTube. Shakir, Yusuf, Magid and six other Muslim scholars appear in a YouTube video[13] – seen by tens of thousands of people – that repudiates violence done in the name of Islam. The video was made in the summer of 2010 by the Muslim Public Affairs Council, after a series of incidents involving young militant American Muslims who said they were – in the name of Islam – retaliating against the United States for its killing of Muslims in Iraq and Afghanistan. In May 2010, for example, 30-year-old Pakistani immigrant Faisal Shahzad – who had been influenced by militants in his former homeland and by radical US cleric Anwar al-Awlaki – tried to detonate a car bomb in New York's Times Square that would have killed dozens of people in a commercial center of the city.

The Muslim Public Affairs Council video – which opens with a headline-like phrase in capital letters, 'Believers Beware: Injustice Cannot Defeat Injustice', was aimed at the American Muslim community and also non-Muslims, to show that Muslim leaders were taking a post-9/11 public stand against violence. Scholars in the video said that militant Muslims like Faisal Shahzad were uneducated and naive.

Imam Suhaib Webb, a white convert from Oklahoma, says in the video:

> In recent months, messages which have been borne from entities outside of this country have encouraged young Muslims in particular and convert Muslims to engage in illegal acts which would not only undermine the security of our country that we live in, our beloved country, and our fellow citizens, but most importantly, ultimately serve to undermine our places in the community and society.

The same month that the Muslim Public Affairs Council released its video on YouTube, a group of 'grass-roots' American Muslims began their own video campaign on YouTube, with students, children, doctors and other working professionals, and Muslims of all backgrounds – including Hispanic and deaf Muslims – volunteering to say that they opposed violence and wanted to integrate peacefully in the United States. Tens of thousands viewed the video and subsequent other videos (including one by a Muslim hip-hop group, Native Deen) uploaded to a website, http://myfaithmyvoice.com, that was started by a video designer in Virginia, David Hawa, who said he was startled by the growing 'Islamophobia' in America. These video campaigns are really part of a media war pitting mainstream American Muslims against the daily torrent of news about Muslims that appear in the mainstream media. It is a media war that may never be declared over. For many mainstream American Muslims, this is the new reality – a long-term effect of 9/11 and the continuing copycat incidents, which now require them to speak up every time someone like Mohamed Osman Mohamud plots to kill innocent people.

Imam Shakir tells me:

> Like most people the overwhelming majority of Muslims are engaged in peaceful pursuits most of the time, so to present the community as inherently violent and aggressive and out to take over the world – there hasn't been an organized Muslim encroachment on a Christian land since the second Ottoman seige of Vienna, and that was over 300 years ago. To present the Muslims as this menace and this new fascism, this new totalitarian menace, is just ridiculous. But when there's a lack of information, and there's a lack of voices coming forward to present an alternative definition, then that starts to take root, especially when you have these periodic episodes such as this thing in Portland that reinforce that image in the minds of a lot of people.

Every Muslim community in America has experienced a level of suspicion that has made them both guarded and open to prove their embrace of peaceful patriotism. In the months before 9/11, I reported on the Afghan community in the Fremont area, visiting mosques and interviewing dozens of people from different backgrounds – from those who were devoutly religious to those who were Muslims in name only. The vast majority of Afghan Muslims in America oppose the form of extremist Islam that was implemented by the Taliban, and in the weeks after 1 October 2001, when the US military began its Afghanistan military attack in response to 9/11 and deposed the Taliban's leadership, including Mullah Mohammed Omar, there were celebrations on the streets of Fremont and a sense that divine justice had been carried out. Similar to Kabul itself, 'Little Kabul' was a place of high hopes. The American dream was being realized, Afghan-Americans said, and they were – for the first time – a public part of it. About 50,000 Afghans live in the San Francisco Bay area, with several thousand in Fremont, where storefronts advertise (in English and Dari) Afghan breads, Afghan clothing, and Afghan books about everything from the bestselling poet Rumi (who was born in Afghanistan) to religious tracts and Quranic readings. To accommodate the growing number of religious Afghans, new mosques have been built in the Fremont area, including the Khalilullah Ibrahim Islamic Center, which opened in 2008 a few minutes' drive from Fremont's City Hall.

'The Bay Area is very much multi-cultural, so people are familiar with other religions and other cultures and people from other countries – but if I go out of this area, and they see I'm an Afghan, they may not like it as much,' Fareed Wardak, a board member of the Islamic center, tells me. Wardak was born in Kabul but immigrated to the United States in 1990 at the age of 21. He recalls the death of Balbir Singh Sodhi, a turban-wearing Sikh-American from India who spent time in the Bay area before moving to Arizona, where he was murdered four days after 9/11 by a man who vowed revenge for the World Trade Center attacks. 'He thought [Balbir Singh] was Muslim,' Wardak says. 'Different areas have different reactions to people.'

Days before I spoke with Wardak, a published report[14] said that the FBI was investigating Afghans in the San Francisco Bay area for ties to Najibullah Zazi, a naturalized citizen from Afghanistan who pleaded guilty in 2010 to planning a suicide bomb attack in New York's subway system. Zazi, who was living in Colorado, had planned to detonate explosives on the nine-year anniversary of 9/11. For many American Muslims, including those from Afghanistan, the post-9/11 wars in Afghanistan and Iraq, and US surveillance of Muslim Americans, amounted to a 'War on Islam', not a 'War on Terror'. Zazi told United States District Court in New York that he undertook his subway operation because, 'I would sacrifice myself to bring attention to what the United States military was doing to civilians in Afghanistan by sacrificing my soul for the sake of saving other souls.'[15] Fawaz Gerges, professor of Middle Eastern politics and international relations at the London School of Economics and Political Science, and the author of *The Rise and Fall of al-Qaeda*, says Zazi's case is an example of 'bottom-up radicalization', where US Muslims volunteer to join al-Qaeda's extremist cause because of their anger at America's military efforts.[16] In *The Rise and Fall of al-Qaeda*, Gerges says young Muslim-American radicals like Zazi become alienated in their adopted countries, then radicalized by 'identity politics' into futile attempts to take innocent lives. But Gerges says the level of 'homegrown terror' is minuscule and gets disproportionate media attention, writing that 'Homegrown extremism is a limited phenomenon and must be kept in perspective. Exaggerated public reports create unnecessary fear.'[17]

For Afghan-Americans and Muslim-Americans in general, the cloud of suspicion that they live under tempers their desire to assimilate into American society. There is no reason to believe these clouds will disappear in the near or long-term future. In some ways, Muslim-Americans are getting used to the condition. They still say they are happy in the United States. In fact, they still insist they would not want to live anywhere else but America. This country, they say, has become their home.

6 The Diversity of American Muslims

A Religious, Ethnic, and Cultural Profile

The al-Farooq Masjid of Atlanta, which cost $10 million to construct and opened in 2008, never fails to dazzle visitors with its architecture. Outside, a sky-scraping minaret and two copper domes – one 80 feet high and 40 feet across, reminiscent of the one that anchors Jerusalem's Dome of the Rock – loom over an octagonal structure with tall entranceways that are framed by classical pointed arches. Inside, the mosque features balconies covered with *mashrabiya* (wood latticework), ivory-colored walls, and columns that elicit the feeling of the Taj Mahal, and rows of intricate windows that let in light from all directions. For many guests, though, the membership of al-Farooq Masjid is equally jaw-dropping. At the main Friday prayer session, which attracts more than 1,000 people, Muslims who were born in Pakistan, India, Somalia, Senegal, France, and other foreign countries pray side by side with Muslims – white, black, and Hispanic – born throughout the United

States, creating a United Nations-like patchwork of ethnicities and backgrounds. Mosque-goers hail originally from more than 30 different nations, so al-Farooq Masjid – besides being one of the biggest mosques in the American southeast – is one of its most diverse.

Other area mosques, although lacking al-Farooq's majestic space, share its diversity. At Masjid Abdullah – a tiny mosque in Lilburn, a city about 20 miles northeast of Atlanta – Muslims from multiple continents who now live in Georgia have made it their primary house of worship. The mosque opened in 2002, one of 35 in the greater Atlanta area.

Both mosques have benefited from the Atlanta area's population growth over the past 30 years (more than 5 million people live there – double the population from 1980), and from their proximity to Atlanta colleges and universities, which number more than 20. Al-Farooq Masjid is just a few blocks north of the Georgia Institute of Technology, and close to downtown Atlanta.

'Thirty years ago, Atlanta was a relatively small place and we were one of two mosques – and this was the international kind of mosque,' Khalid Siddiq, an endocrinologist who sits on the board of al-Farooq Masjid, tells me. Siddiq, who's originally from Pakistan, says,

A lot of students at Georgia Tech did come from different countries, from various ethnic backgrounds, and there were also people from the Middle East at Lockheed (a large aerospace company with an operation in Atlanta) and other companies – so there was this diversity of the origin of people coming to the mosque. And that is why we [continue to] have an unusually large number of different nationalities that come to the mosque.

The most diverse Muslim community in the world lives in the United States. Muslims from at least 68 different nations reside in America, according to a major 2007 poll, *Muslim Americans: Middle Class and Mostly Mainstream*, released by the Pew Research Center.[1] Of these foreign-born Muslim immigrants, the greatest number (37 percent) is from the Arab world.[2] The next-highest number of immigrant Muslims in America (27 percent) is from South Asia – mainly Pakistan (almost half the total of South Asians), India (almost a quarter of the total), Bangladesh, and Afghanistan.[3] Next is Iran (12 percent of Muslim-American immigrants were born there), Europe (8 percent), and Sub-Saharan African countries (6 percent).[4] A disparate range of other countries and regions compose the final 10 percent of immigrant American Muslims. Almost two-thirds of American Muslims, 65 percent, were born abroad, the poll said.[5]

Of the 35 percent of American Muslims who were born in the United States, a little more than half are African-American, according to the Pew poll.[6] Among all US Muslims, African-Americans make up 20 percent of the population.[7] More than a third of American Muslims (38 percent) identify themselves as white, 20 percent as Asian, and 16 percent as 'other or mixed race'.[8] Hispanics – whether white Hispanics or black Hispanics – compose 4 percent of American Muslims, according to the poll.[9]

Every Muslim denomination, including Sufi and Ahmadiyya, can be found in the United States in relatively large numbers, but Sunni Islam – the dominant faith among Muslims worldwide – is the most widespread in the United States, with 50 percent of American Muslims saying they are Sunni, according to the Pew poll.[10] Sixteen percent are Shia, with 5 percent saying they are another Muslim faith, such as that of the Nation of Islam.[11] Twenty-two percent of those surveyed didn't specify a particular denomination, while 7 percent didn't respond at all to the question.[12]

Another major poll of American Muslims, this one released in 2009 by the Gallup Center for Muslim Studies, revealed slightly different numbers. In the Gallup survey, for example, African-Americans make up the largest bloc of US Muslims, at 35 percent.[13] The next-biggest bloc, 28 percent, was those identifying themselves as 'white', followed by Asians at 18 percent.[14] One percent of American Muslims are Hispanic.[15] Eighteen percent of those responding to Gallup's survey selected 'Other' – a choice that 'may reflect identification with more than one race or people's discomfort with conventional racial categories', according to the poll.[16] (Gallup, whose poll was titled *Muslim Americans: A National Portrait*, questioned interviewees from a cross-section of random households – Muslim and non-Muslim – and then analyzed both categories' responses. By contrast, the Pew survey specifically targeted Muslim respondents.) A third poll of US Muslims, from Zogby International in 2004, paralleled the Pew results, finding that 64 percent of American Muslims were foreign-born,[17] and that, overall, a large number of Muslims are South Asian in origin (30 percent), Arab (26 percent), and African-American (20 percent).[18] A 2001 Zogby poll said Muslim-Americans hailed from at least 79 countries outside the United States.[19]

One of the biggest questions, 'How many Muslims live in America?', was addressed by the Pew survey, which estimated 2.35 million[20] – a number it said represented 'perhaps the most rigorous effort to date to scientifically estimate the size of the Muslim American population.'[21] Most major US Muslim organizations claim there are at least 6 million American Muslims and as many as 9 million. A 2011 survey of US mosques, 'The American Mosque 2011', for example, found that 2.6 million

Muslims were associated with American mosques, and that factoring in Muslims who were unaffiliated with mosques boosted the overall total to between 6 million and 7 million.[22] The first serious estimate of American Muslims, done in 1960 by the Federation of Islamic Associations, put the figure at 1.2 million.[23] In 2008, the American Religious Identification Survey said there were 1.34 million Muslims in the United States.[24]

The differing numbers reflect the polling groups' different survey methods – and the lack of official government data on faith. The United States doesn't ask its citizens about their religions, a policy that dates back to 1791, to the First Amendment of the Constitution, which is designed to keep the government from advocating or imposing a religious belief on Americans. The amendment's directive ('Congress shall make no law respecting an establishment of religion') was meant, Thomas Jefferson noted in 1802, to put a 'wall of separation between church and state'. Over 200 years later, the wall remains, but America's religious complexion has changed dramatically. The vast majority of Americans still follow Christianity: according to the *American Religious Identification Survey*, 76 percent of Americans identify with some denomination of Christianity, topped by Catholicism – with 25.1 percent, or 57 million Americans – and then the Baptist faith, with 15.8 percent, or 36 million Americans.[25] (Other polls list Protestants as the biggest Christian group in America.[26]) In the last 20 years, however, non-Christian faiths have experienced the biggest growth among American religions. The number of Muslims in the United States has more than doubled since 1990, according to the *American Religious Identification Survey*,[27] making Islam one of the United States' fastest-growing religions. Most religious surveys of Americans say Islam is one of the biggest non-Christian religions in the country. In 2007, for example, the

Pew Forum's *U.S. Religious Landscape Survey* said Islam was the third-largest religion among non-Christian faiths, at 0.6 percent of the population, behind Buddhism (second, with 0.7 percent of American adults claiming the religion) and Judaism (with 1.7 percent of Americans identifying as Jewish.)[28]

For Muslim-Americans, their growth in the United States is both a source of pride and a source of confusion since it's unclear exactly where they stand in relation to other religions' populations. What is clear is that they are more visible today than ever before – politically, culturally, and religiously – with multiple mosques in every major American city and mosques in every state; with Muslim-American leaders more visible in the media and on Capitol Hill; with Muslim-Americans of every denomination and ethnic background living across the United States; with second- and third-generation Muslims advocating everything from religious liberalism to a return to strict Islamic traditions; and with secular, feminist, and even gay and lesbian Muslims finding a home for their activism where one wouldn't exist in their native lands – Islam has established itself in America in a way that is different from any country in the world.

What follows is an overview of the different denominations, geographic origins, and other key traits that make American Islam so distinctive.

Mosques

The number of US mosques has steadily increased in the past two decades, and there are now 2,106 – a 74 percent increase since the year 2000, when there were 1,209 Muslim houses of worship, according to *The American Mosque 2011*, a study done by a coalition of organizations, including the Council on

American-Islamic Relations.[29] Seventy-six percent of America's mosques have been built since 1980, says the report,[30] which found that the city with the highest number of mosques was New York, with 192.[31] *The American Mosque 2011* found high levels of diversity. The highest percentage of US mosque-goers are South Asian (33 percent), followed by Arab (27 percent), African-American (24 percent), Sub-Saharan African (9 percent), European (2 percent), White (1 percent), Caribbean (1 percent), Southeast Asian (1 percent), Latino (1 percent), and Turkish (1 percent).[32] Just 3 percent of American mosques have only one ethnic group that attends that mosque.[33] At Islam's most important prayer gathering, the Friday *jumu'ah* prayer, an average of 353 people attend each US mosque, compared to an average of 292 in 2000 and 150 in 1994.[34]

Sunni and Shia Islam

While half of all US Muslims say they are Sunni Muslims, those most likely to be Sunni are Muslim-Americans with roots in Pakistan or another South Asian country, according to the Pew report *Muslim Americans: Middle Class and Mostly Mainstream*.[35] The least likely to be Sunni are African-American Muslims and Iranian-American Muslims.[36] While 16 percent of American Muslims are Shia,[37] most Iranian-American Muslims (91 percent) follow the denomination,[38] according to *Muslim Americans: Middle Class and Mostly Mainstream*.

The distinction between Sunni and Shia – which centers on the historical leadership succession to the Prophet Muhammad, and has frequently led to bloody confrontations in the Middle East – is less pronounced in the United States, where Sunni and Shia Muslims frequently pray side by side in the same mosques.

Marriages between Sunni and Shia also take place in the United States. Still, division between Sunni and Shia – the two most prominent Muslim denominations in the world – exists in America. Muslim organizations commonly label mosques as 'Sunni' or 'Shia', and organizations that promote each denomination are prominent in the United States. Sects within each denomination have US followers, including the Ismaili community of Shia, who are most visible through the work of the Aga Khan, the Ismailis' spiritual leader (and a descendant of the Prophet Muhammad), who frequently travels from his home in Europe to make US appearances, as he did in November 2011 when he signed a public agreement between the state of Illinois and Ismaili institutions to collaborate on social-work projects in Illinois. Ismaili Muslims, who numbered just a few hundred in the United States 50 years ago,[39] now are in the tens of thousands,[40] and have *jamatkhana*, where they hold prayer sessions and meetings, throughout the United States.

Sufi Islam

Tens of thousands of people in the United States are active followers of Sufism,[41] the mystical branch of Islam that first gained an American following from 1910 to 1912, when Hazrat Inayat Khan, a Sufi Muslim musician from India, traveled around the United States promoting his vision of tolerance and universal brotherhood. An American grandson of Inayat Khan, Pir Zia Inayat-Khan, leads the Sufi Order International, which Inayat Khan founded. The order is one of many Sufi orders, or *tariqas*, that are prominent in the United States. Many of them – including the Naqshbandi-Nazimiyya Sufi Order of America, which is led by a Lebanese-born scholar, Muhammad Hisham

Kabbani – stress traditional Islamic beliefs but emphasize mystical rituals such as dhikr, where followers repeat words of Islamic devotion while doing physical worship, which can be expressed by jumping, dancing, or even twirling. Like Sufi orders around the world, US orders revolve around a *sheikh*, or leader, who is trained in Sufi traditions, but some US Sufi orders do not require its members to be Muslim, and many orders conduct their meetings outside of mosques – including in churches. Sufism has gained a larger foothold in the United States in the past 20 years, dovetailing with the growing popularity of Sufi poetry. One of America's bestselling poets is Jalaluddin Rumi, the thirteenth-century Sufi mystic, whose US books have sold more than 500,000 copies in the past 30 years thanks to translations by Coleman Barks, a retired professor at the University of Georgia who translates Rumi's words into what Barks told me is 'language that is more in the tradition of American free verse of spiritual, searching poetry. We have a tradition that is known throughout the world for its elegance and delicacy and its plain-spokenness.'[42] Typical of US Sufi orders is the Nur Ashki Jerrahi Community, based in New York City, which – started by US Sufi converts and associated with the Halveti-Jerrahi Order of Dervishes in Turkey – welcomes people of 'all religious and non-religious paths' to its ceremonies.[43]

Nation of Islam

About 50,000 people are members of the Nation of Islam,[44] which once claimed hundreds of thousands of members at its height of popularity in the 1960s (when Malcolm X was a member) and early 1970s. From its beginnings in the early 1930s, the Nation of Islam has practiced a radically unorthodox version of Islam, stressing that its members – who are all African-American – try to live completely separate from white Americans. Ultimately, the Nation of Islam believes, black Americans deserve their own nation – funded and supported by white Americans whose ancestors enslaved Africans for generations. The Nation of Islam says that its founder, Wallace Fard Muhammad, was God himself, and that Wallace Fard Muhammad was both the Christian Messiah and the Muslim *Mahdi* – the person put on Earth to redeem people before the Day of Judgment. In 1975, Warith Deen Muhammad took over from his father and guided most of the Nation's members to Sunni Islam while changing the name of the organization. Louis Farrakhan then revitalized the Nation of Islam, keeping most of the original ideologies.

Other Muslim Denominations

Similar to the Nation of Islam, the Moorish Science Temple of America began in the early twentieth century as a faith for African-Americans. Its founder, Noble Drew Ali, said African-Americans were descended from Moroccans and were really Asiatic 'Moorish' people, and they should adhere to a religion that incorporated Islam. Ali, who was born and raised in North Carolina, referred to Islam as Mohammedanism. The temple, started in 1925, has its male members wear fezzes, and all its members refer to themselves as Moors and take as part of their surname the name 'Bey' or 'El'. Tens of thousands of Americans belonged to the Moorish Science Temple in the 1930s,[45] but its membership is now in the hundreds. Other minor sects (including a group called the Nation of Gods and Earths, or the Five Percenters) exist that appeal to African-Americans and promote the message that what they say is a variation of Islam.

The Ahmadiyya Muslim Community – which believes that the group's founder, Mirza Ghulam Ahmad, was a prophet and the Islamic Mahdi – was founded in India and based in the United Kingdom but also has a following in the United States, claiming more than 60 chapters around the country and thousands of members.[46] The Ahmadiyya, who believe in a strict separation of church and state, established themselves in the United States in 1920, when one of its disciples, Muhammad Sadiq, arrived from India to preach his faith for three years. Sadiq converted 700 people in that time,[47] when he became one of the first Muslim missionaries from abroad to preach Islam in the United States.

Wahhabism, a strict interpretation of Islam that began in Saudi Arabia in the eighteenth century, has adherents in the United States, as do other extremist versions of Islam, including the ideologies put forward by the Muslim Brotherhood, which began in Egypt in 1928. In a 2011 poll taken by the Pew Research Center's Global Attitudes Project, 15 percent of Muslim-Americans said there was a 'fair amount' of support for extremism amongst Muslim-Americans, while 6 percent of those surveyed said that there was a 'great deal' of support for extremism.[48] Asked if suicide bombing and other violence against civilians were ever justified 'to defend Islam from its enemies', 1 percent of American Muslims said the actions were 'often' justified, 7 percent said 'sometimes', and 5 percent said 'rarely', with 78 percent saying 'never'.[49] This minority/majority split, where a small percentage hold extremist views, was reflected in *The American Mosque 2011* poll, which found that just 1 percent of US mosque leaders take 'a Salafi approach' to Islam, which emphasizes the earliest interpretations of the religion, while 11 percent follow traditional legal schools of thought that were first practiced centuries ago.[50] Saudi Arabia has funded at least 15 mosques or Islamic centers in the United States, including the

$8.1 million King Fahad Mosque in Culver City, California,[51] where two of the 9/11 hijackers, Saudi nationals Khalid al-Mihdhar and Nawaf al-Hazmi, attended services while living in California in the months before the 2001 terrorist attacks.[52]

Arab-American Muslims

Twenty-six percent of Muslim-Americans are of Arab descent, according to the Zogby International poll,[53] while the Pew study says 24 percent of all US Muslims are of Arab descent, with 37 percent of foreign-born American Muslims from Arab countries.[54] Muslim Arabs are most prominent in the Detroit suburb of Dearborn, making up somewhat less than 30 percent of the city's 100,000 residents. In the early twentieth century, Christian and Muslim Arabs from the Middle East began immigrating to the Detroit/Dearborn area in great numbers to work in the automobile factories. With subsequent waves of immigration – especially in the late 1970s from Lebanon, when that country was experiencing civil war, and the 1980s and 1990s from Iraq, when that country was in turmoil – Dearborn became the city with America's highest Arab concentration. The United States' largest mosque, the Islamic Center of America – a 120,000-square- foot complex that cost $14 million to construct – is located in Dearborn, a short ride from the headquarters of the Ford Motor Company.

Among Arab-Americans, those of Lebanese ancestry predominate, representing 30 percent of the total, according to US census figures from 2000 that were analyzed by the Arab American Institute.[55] Second in terms of numbers are Egyptian-Americans and Syrian-Americans, who respectively account for 12 percent and 9 percent of all Arab-Americans.[56] Americans of

Palestinian ancestry are the fourth-most populous group (at 6 percent), followed by Americans of Iraqi and Moroccan ancestry (both at 5 percent).[57] According to the 2000 census, 1.19 million Americans claim at least some Arab ancestry.[58] Though these totals only take into account ancestry – not religious affiliation – they may loosely reflect the proportional totals of Arab-American Muslims. Lebanese Muslims, for example, have been among America's earliest and steadiest immigrant groups, and in 1934 helped found the 'Mother Mosque' – the United States' first permanent Muslim house of worship – in Cedar Rapids, Iowa.

African-American Muslims

Two out of every 10 Muslims in the United States are African-American, and almost six out of every 10 converts to Islam in the United States are African-American, says the Pew Research Center report, *Muslim Americans: Middle Class and Mostly Mainstream*.[59] Seven percent of American Muslims are from Africa, according to the 2004 poll by Zogby International.[60] Africans, in fact, are among the fastest-growing segments of the American Muslim community. In New York, for example, West African Muslims have opened a number of new mosques that emphasize Sufi (tariqa) traditions from their countries.

Pakistani-American Muslims

Of those Muslim-Americans who were born in another country, 12 percent have come from Pakistan, according to the Pew Research Center report.[61] Overall, Pakistani-Americans make up 8 percent of American Muslims,[62] and are generally better off compared to other Muslims. According to the Pew report, 68 percent of Pakistani-American Muslims say their personal financial situation is 'excellent' or 'good', in contrast to those of Arab descent (42 percent checking 'excellent' or 'good') and African-Americans (30 percent saying their finances were 'excellent' or 'good').[63]

Iranian-American Muslims

Iranian-Americans make up 8 percent of all American Muslims, according to the Pew Research Center report,[64] which says they are overwhelmingly (91 percent) Shia.[65] Though Iranian-American Muslims are scattered around the United States, their biggest presence is in southern California, where in Los Angeles – close to UCLA, on Westwood Boulevard – rows of storefronts promote Iranian culture and religion in an area known as 'Tehrangeles'. The Iranian-American Muslim Association of North America, the most prominent organization for Iranian-American Muslims, is located in Los Angeles.

Afghan-Americans Muslims

Two percent of American Muslims are from Afghanistan, according to the 2004 poll by Zobgy International.[66] Afghans began arriving in large numbers after the Soviet invasion of their country in 1979, and Afghanistan's decades-long turmoil has continued to boost the number of immigrants into the hundreds of thousands. Afghan-American communities are prominent in Virginia, New York, and California – particularly the San Francisco Bay area, home to 'Little Kabul' in Fremont, California.

European-American Muslims

Five percent of American Muslims were born in Europe, according to the Pew Research Center report.[67] New immigrants are from such countries as Bosnia and Herzegovina, Albania, and Bulgaria, but European Muslims were among the early immigrants to America. In 1928, for example, Polish Muslims established a mosque in Brooklyn, New York, that was used for decades.

Convert American Muslims

One-fifth of American Muslims are converts, according to Zogby International's 2004 survey, 'Muslims in the American Public Square'.[68] Each US mosque oversees 15 conversions a year, which would put the annual number of American conversions to Islam at 32,000, according to *The American Mosque 2011* survey.[69] African-Americans make up almost three-fifths (59 percent) of converts, according to the Pew study, which says most converts (81 percent) are those who formerly identified as Christians.[70] Fifteen percent said they had no religion before converting.[71] Four percent of American Muslims are of Hispanic origin or descent, says the Pew Research Center report.[72] The conversion of Hispanic-Americans is a relatively new phenomenon in the United States, with at least 50,000 converts in the last 10 years, according to US Muslim leaders.[73]

Secular Muslim Americans

Non-practicing Muslims are a significant minority in America. Eighteen percent of American Muslims never attend mosque services,[74] 16 percent say they seldom attend,[75] and 12 percent say they never pray,[76] according to Pew's *Muslim Americans: Middle Class and Mostly Mainstream.* (Forty-one percent of American Muslims do the five prayers that are obligated by orthodox Islam.[77]) New York state is the headquarters for the Institution for the Secularization of Islamic Society, which was started by secular Muslims (and secular non-Muslims). The group advocates a 'secular state that does not endorse any religion, religious institution, or any religious dogma',[78] and its main goal is to 'create a network of secularists and freethinkers in Islamic countries'.[79] In the months after 9/11, the *New York Times* reported on secular Muslims, interviewing a Pakistan-born Muslim in Los Angeles, Khalid Pervaiz, who – with two young daughters – was celebrating Christmas, complete with a tree that had an angel on top. 'Every once in a blue moon I will go for my Friday prayers,' Pervaiz told the paper, 'but I still think I'm a good Muslim. If I don't go and pray five times a day, I don't think I'm less of a Muslim. I'm just not a practicing, going-to-the-masjid Muslim.'[80] In the 2009 study by the Gallup Center for Muslim Studies, 10 percent of respondents said they had consumed 4–5 drinks of alcohol in the past 1–4 days, with 4 percent of respondents saying they had 4–5 drinks in the previous 5–7 days.[81] Drinking any alcohol is prohibited in Islam.

Gay and Lesbian Muslim Americans

In 1998 in Boston, Faisal Alam – who was raised in Connecticut after spending his first 10 years in Pakistan – started an organization, called al-Fatiha, for Muslims who are gay, lesbian, bisexual, transgender, intersex, or questioning their gender or orientation. Al-Fatiha's launch in Boston – at an event reported to be the first public gathering of self-identified gay and lesbian Muslims[82] – has led to eight US chapters being formed and seven affiliated organizations in Canada, Great Britain, and South Africa.[83] Eight hundred people belong to al-Fatiha. One member, Daayiee Abdullah, who is believed to be the only openly gay imam in the United States, says there is nothing in the Quran or the Sunnah that prohibits homosexuality, telling one interviewer, 'The Koran does not say that same-sex individuals should not have loving relationships.'[84] In Islam, sexual relations between men are strictly prohibited, based on Islamic tradition and interpretations of the Quran and the sayings of the Prophet Muhammad. The Islamic term to describe homosexuality, *liwat*, is related to the people of Lut (Sodom and Gomorrah), who – in the Quran – are condemned by God because of their sexual misdeeds.

State by State

Muslims are concentrated in the country's largest states and cosmopolitan areas, according to a 2001 *American Religious Identification Survey* done by the City University of New York's Graduate Center. New York state has the most Muslim-Americans (24 percent), followed by Illinois (10 percent), California (9 percent), Texas (9 percent), Michigan (6 percent), New Jersey (5 percent), and (with 4 percent each) Ohio, Maryland, Georgia, and Virginia.[85]

Eighty percent of American Muslims say that religion plays an important part in their life, according to *Muslim Americans: A National Portrait*, the 2009 study by the Gallup Center for Muslim Studies.[86] Among major religions polled by Gallup in the United States, only Mormons have more enthusiasm for their faith, with 85 percent saying religion is important to them.[87] More than a third of American Muslims (41 percent) go to the mosque at least once a week, Gallup's survey says.[88] Almost half of all US Muslims (49 percent) perform the five daily prayers required for fully observant Muslims, according to Zogby International's 2004 poll, 'Muslims in the American Public Square'.[89] *The American Mosque 2011* survey found that mosque attendance had increased by 20 percent from the previous 10 years.[90] However, other studies have found lesser levels of faith among American Muslims, producing a contradictory portrait of Islam in America. For example, Pew's *Muslim Americans: Middle Class and Mostly Mainstream*, found that 34 percent of American Muslims 'seldom' or 'never' attend mosque,[91] and that 60 percent of American Muslims believe 'there is more than one true way to interpret the teachings of Islam.'[92]

Almost half (43 percent) of those responding to Pew's survey said that Muslims who newly arrive in the United States should adopt American customs.[93] Almost the same amount (42 percent) said their personal financial situation was 'excellent/ good', with 52 percent saying it was 'fair/poor'.[94] Sixty-two percent said that, for women, life was better in the United States than it was in Muslim countries.[95] And almost half of Muslim Americans (47 percent) say they consider themselves as 'Muslim' first before 'American',[96] although in Great Britain the number of Muslims who think of themselves as Muslim first before 'British' is 81 percent.[97]

All these statistics paint a complex portrait of American Muslims, who don't fit into one easy category. Among religious groups, Muslims are the most racially diverse in America. Intermarriage between Muslims and non-Muslims was (and is) common in the United States. In the mid twentieth century, for example, immigrants from Yemen who worked as farm laborers in California married Hispanic-Americans who didn't convert to Islam. The Pew report stated that 62 percent of American Muslims say it is 'okay' for a Muslim to marry a non-Muslim[98] – a level of acceptance that does not exist in Muslim-majority countries.

In 2003, the Iranian-American scholar Vartan Gregorian wrote a book called *Islam: A Mosaic, Not a Monolith*, which detailed the religion's history and complexity – and included the observation that Muslims in America 'must resolve to become an integral part of the social fabric of the United States'.[99] Gregorian also said that America had to do better at accepting its Muslim citizens and their religion – that 'there is a disconnect between [Americans'] passions about Islam and our knowledge of it.'[100] This parallel narrative – the need for more understanding and the need for more integration – has been fundamental to American Islam from the beginning. Polls and numbers offer one perspective of American Islam. People – individuals and the organizations that represent them – offer another context that's essential to understanding Islam in America.

7 Who's Who in Muslim America

'The Muslims in America are utterly divided; there is no single voice for them.'[1] These are the words of Mike Ghouse, a Muslim-American writer and activist from Dallas, Texas, whose observations are shared by many other American Muslims. Whenever a major controversy arises for them, such as the one in 2010 about the appropriateness of an Islamic center near the World Trade Center towers in New York, a cacophony of voices floods the media and public forums – leaving people to wonder whose voice really matters for Muslim Americans. One answer: 'It depends.' Muslim-American leaders whose religious teachings and political views are considered to be 'moderate' have large followings in the United States. But other leaders who dispense a more conservative view of Islam, and are more rigid in their political views, also have many platforms from which to influence American Muslims. And even Muslims who might have been marginalized before the age of the internet – Muslims who are liberal, radical, secular, comedic, untrained in Islamic theology, or uninterested in opposing views – now have a way to persuade other American Muslims with their arguments and video clips.

The most influential Muslim-Americans have one thing in common with the organizations that seek to speak for Muslim-Americans: they are all relatively young, if not in age then in the years they've been in the spotlight. The Islamic Society of North America, for example, is rooted in the early 1960s, when the Muslim Students Association was founded in the American Midwest, but it has really only established itself as a formidable force – with highly attended conferences, meetings at the White House with the president, and other levels of outreach – in the past 15 years. The panorama of American Islam is reflected in the faces of the people and organizations that are profiled here.

People

Akbar S. Ahmed: The former Pakistan ambassador to Great Britain is now one of America's most authoritative voices on Islam, advising the US government on the religion and acting as both an outside observer of American Islam and an inside practitioner. Ahmed is the Ibn Khaldun Chair of Islamic Studies at American University in Washington, DC, and the First Distinguished Chair of Middle East and Islamic Studies at the US Naval Academy. Considered a progressive Muslim, Ahmed nevertheless offers views that counter those of other progressive American Muslims, as when he came out against the Islamic center proposed for an area near New York's 'Ground Zero', the site of the towers that were brought down by the 9/11 hijackers. Ahmed said the center's proponents – including Feisal Abdul Rauf, a New York imam – failed to recognize the insensitivity of putting a high-profile Islamic center so close to the spot where thousands of people were brutally killed. He says US Muslim leaders are partly to blame for Americans' general lack of understanding of Islam. 'Most Americans, even after 9/11 when there are such important reasons to understand Islam, really have the foggiest idea of Islam,' he said in a 2010 interview with journalist Sally Quinn at Georgetown University in the nation's capital.[2] 'The reasons are two-fold [but] No. 1 is the failure of Muslim leadership [...] As a community, they failed to make an impact on America.'

Muhammad Ali: One of America's most famous converts to Islam, Ali was raised a Baptist but converted to Islam in 1964, first adopting the beliefs of the Nation of Islam, then in 1975 embracing Sunni Islam after the Nation's separatist views were swept aside by Warith Deen Muhammad. A three-time world heavyweight boxing champion, Ali was diagnosed in 1984 with Parkinson's disease, and has in more recent years embraced Sufism; he still affirms, in public, his identity as a Muslim. His daughter, Hana Yasmeen Ali, told an interviewer in 2008[3] that Ali became attracted to Sufism after reading the works of Hazrat Inayat Khan, an Indian Muslim who preached Sufism in the United States in 1910. 'My father is very spiritual – more spiritual now than he is religious,' Hana said.[4]

> It was important for him to be very religious and take the stands he did in earlier years. It was a different time. He still tries to convert people to Islam but it's not the same. His health and his spirituality have changed, and it's not so much about being religious, but about going out and making people happy, doing charity, and supporting people and causes.

Throughout his life, Ali expressed his faith as much in terms of politics and culture as about religion, saying in 1977

– during a public question-and-answer session in England[5] – that he adopted Islam in the early 1960s at a time when racial segregation was still an issue in the United States. He said:

> I choose to follow the Islamic path because I never saw so much love, I never saw so many people hugging each other, kissing each other, praying five times a day [...] You can go to any country and say, 'Salaam aleykum', 'Alaykum salaam', and you got a home, you got a brother. I chose the Islamic path because it connected me. As a Christian in America, I couldn't go to the white churches. That was for those people. It did them good.[6]

Other well-known sports figures who converted to Islam include Kareem Abdul-Jabbar (the former Lew Alcindor), who starred in the National Basketball Association, and boxer Mike Tyson.

Imam Muhammad Shamsi Ali: After religious training in his native Indonesia and then in Pakistan and teaching in Saudi Arabia, Ali immigrated in 1996 to the United States, where he is chairman of the al-Hikmah Mosque in Queens, which is the only one in the greater New York area devoted to the Indonesian-American community. The community has grown in size as more people from Indonesia, the world's most populous Muslim nation, have settled in the United States. Ali, who speaks fluent English, Arabic, Urdu, and Indonesian, is a strong advocate of interfaith work, and his initiatives – like leading delegations to New York synagogues – have been applauded by many Muslim-Americans, and lambasted by others. Ali, the former imam at the Islamic Cultural Center of New York, the largest mosque in Manhattan, said to al-Jazeera,

In the beginning I had just 10 people who came with me [to visit a synagogue]. But the following year I have like 30 people. The next year not only did they want to come, even they asked when we are going to visit the synagogue. So changes are taking place in the Muslim community.[7]

Reza Aslan: Born in Iran in 1972, Aslan has become a much-quoted authority on Islam after the publication of his 2005 book, *No God but God: The Origins, Evolution, and Future of Islam.* What makes Aslan's written work stand out is its mix of narrative writing, personal anecdotes, occasional humor, reportage, and historical analysis. An associate professor of creative writing at the University of California at Riverside, Aslan has an undergraduate degree in religion from Santa Clara University, a master's in theological studies from Harvard Divinity School, and a masters in fiction from the University of Iowa. Aslan has told me that American Muslims can be role models for a more 'tolerant' Islam[8] – a point he also made to an interviewer in 2005, when he said,

I believe we are living in the time of the Islamic reformation. In fact, I think we are living in the twilight of that reformation [...] [Islam is] adapting itself to the realities of the world around it. I think we'll see the same process we saw in the Christian reformation from doctrinal absolutism to doctrinal relativism; toward a truly indigenous Islamic enlightenment. And it's up to us as Muslims in the US to give voice to that for our brothers and sisters who don't have the voice or the same ability to speak out as we do.[9]

Khaled Abou El Fadl: A law professor at the University of California at Los Angeles and an observant Muslim who has memorized the Quran, Abou El Fadl is an authority on Islamic law. Through his many media appearances, he has become the face of a moderate vision of Islam that rejects, on legal and moralistic grounds, all violence done in the name of Islam – particularly the extremism carried out by Osama bin Laden and his lieutenant Ayman al-Zawahiri, the former doctor who, like Abou El Fadl, is from Egypt. Abou El Fadl, who was also raised in Kuwait, has a law degree from the University of Pennsylvania Law School, and a master's and doctorate in Islamic law from Princeton University. Abou El Fadl often addresses the subject of biases and stereotypes against Muslims, and developments in Islam that have led extremist elements to employ violence and justifying their actions on *hadiths* (sayings of the Prophet Muhammad), Quranic implorations, or legal rulings of ambivalent truth. 'We must have the will power and courage', Abou El Fadl writes in his 2005 book, *The Great Theft: Wrestling Islam from the Extremists*, 'to reclaim and re-establish Islam as a humanistic moral force in the world today.'[10]

Keith Ellison: An African-American convert to Islam, Ellison became, in 2007, the first Muslim elected to the US Congress. Ellison, who converted from Catholicism as a 19-year-old in college, was re-elected in 2010 from his Minnesota district, which is the state's most ethnically diverse district and includes the city of Minneapolis – the biggest urban area in Minnesota. In Congress, Ellison has authored legislation on tax credits for homeless youth, protecting tenants from foreclosure, and other 'liberal' issues. He advocated that the United States reduce its military and financial involvement in wars in Iraq and Afghanistan, but has generally refrained from offering his opinions in Congress about religion or Islam. Just before his inauguration in 2007, Ellison told an interfaith group in Detroit,

'I'm not a religious leader, I've never led religious services of any kind. I'm not here to be a preacher, but in terms of political agenda items, my faith informs me.'[11] At the swearing-in ceremony in Congress, Ellison – instead of using a Bible that members would traditionally use – put his hand on a Quran that had been owned by Thomas Jefferson. 'It demonstrates', said Ellis, 'that from the very beginning of our country, we had people who were visionary, who were religiously tolerant, who believed that knowledge and wisdom could be gleaned from any number of sources, including the Quran.'[12]

Muhammad Hisham Kabbani: The leader of a Sufi community, the Naqshbandi-Nazimiyya Sufi Order of America, which is based in Michigan and has 23 centers in North America, Kabbani was born and raised in Lebanon and educated in Europe and the Middle East before moving to the United States in 1991. Kabbani's order traces its lineage indirectly to Abu Bakr, Islam's first caliph and the father-in-law of the Prophet Muhammad. Like other Sufi groups, the Naqshbandi-Nazimiyya Sufi Order of America asks its adherents to study Islam under a master (sheikh) and to participate in dhikr ceremonies of public praying, which can take place in many venues. Kabbani, who has a degree in Islamic law from Syria, has met regularly with US government leaders, including – in 2006 – vice president Dick Cheney. Kabbani has publicly criticized what he says is radicalism in American mosques. Kabbani started a group called the Islamic Supreme Council of America, whose mission includes holding interfaith meetings. 'We present a historically authentic version of Islam,' Kabbani has said.

The Prophet Muhammad always extended his hand to all people, regardless of their beliefs, and so do we [...] We live in the United States, a country where people generally are very open to learning about other faiths and cultures. We Muslims must reciprocate by sharing our faith in a way that others may understand and appreciate, without being close-minded or insensitive to their beliefs.[13]

Michael Muhammad Knight: An Irish-American convert to Islam, Knight wrote the 2003 novel *The Taqwacores*, about a Muslim punk-rock scene in Buffalo, New York. The fictional work – whose name incorporates the Arabic word *taqwa*, or 'God consciousness', with the suffix that is often associated with 'hardcore' – imagines a group of Muslim students with Mohawks and other punk-rock predilections who are also deeply religious. The novel, which Knight has said was partly based on real characters, inspired a group of real-life American Muslims to form *Taqwacore* bands that now tour the United States and abroad. A documentary about the bands and Knight was made, as was a dramatic adaptation of the book. Knight, who converted to Islam after reading the autobiography of Malcolm X and studied Islam in Pakistan, has a graduate degree in Islamic studies at Harvard University. Knight's irreverence and rebellious behavior have turned off some Muslim-Americans and attracted others. In explaining why he left the group called the Progressive Muslim Union of North America, Knight wrote on his blog:

For me, the scene just comes off as a lame attempt to reframe the Prophet within modern liberalism, stretch the traditions, and make Islam a little more slack, softer, more huggable. That's not my game. I can endorse woman-led prayer without the need of a scholar telling me that it's okay and has precedents from the Prophet's life. If the Prophet wouldn't have liked it, then in 2005 the Prophet is wrong, *&^% on him. La ilaha illa Allah.[14]

(For more on Muslim punk-rock music in America, see Chapter 10.)

John Walker Lindh: Raised in Maryland and California, Lindh made international headlines in December 2001 after he was captured in Afghanistan, where he had met Osama bin Laden and joined Taliban forces in their fight against troops of the Northern Alliance and, subsequently, the US-led military. Lindh, who converted to Islam as a teenager in 1997, was dubbed 'American Taliban' by the American media. Under the terms of his incarceration and 20-year sentence, Lindh cannot speak to the media nor convey any words to outsiders – whether about his prison conditions, his views of Islam, or anything else – but updates of his life regularly appear in the media, as in December 2010, when his lawyer sued the Federal Bureau of Prisons to allow group prayers for Muslims at the Federal Correctional Complex, Terre Haute (in Indiana), where Lindh is being held. Lindh, who has changed his name to Abu Sulayman al-Irlandi, reportedly submitted three poems in 2010 to a website that reports on prisoners being held at the US facility in Guantánamo Bay, Cuba.[15] The poems include one that's a homage to Guantánamo prisoner Omar Khadr (the youngest combatant to be taken there), which features the concluding stanza:[16]

> I end with a message to every oppressor
> To each gavel-grasping bench-squatting cross-dresser
> As you judge you'll be judged and my closing remark is
> A victory jig on the back of your carcass

On the internet, Lindh's poems have been praised by Muslim readers, and at least one website has been created to argue that Lindh's sentence and plea deal were too harsh given his crimes.[17]

Ingrid Mattson: The first woman and first convert to lead the Islamic Center of North America – the continent's largest Muslim organization – Mattson has spoken out on issues related to Islam and women, saying she has a 'conservative' approach to the issue.[18] For example, she advocates against mosques excluding women from prayer but says that activists should work from a theological standpoint in convincing reticent Muslims, and that individual preferences about prayer spaces – no matter how repugnant to others – need to be respected. 'To have solidarity among women, we do not need to have a utopian sisterhood, where all women are joined in a mystical bond of love and caring,' Mattson has said.[19] Mattson, who has a doctorate in Near Eastern languages and civilizations from the University of Chicago, ended her tenure as ISNA president in 2010. Now at Canada's University of Western Ontario, she continues to speak around the United States after leaving her position in 2012 as professor of Islamic studies and director of Islamic chaplaincy at the Macdonald Center for Islamic Studies and Christian–Muslim Relations at Hartford Seminary in Hartford, Connecticut.

Dalia Mogahed: A former advisor on Muslim affairs to the administration of Barack Obama and former executive director of the Gallup Center for Muslim Studies, Mogahed directs a Washington, DC consultancy that advises governments and organizations, and she is a frequent lecturer and media interviewee. Mogahed is co-author of the 2007 book *Who Speaks for Islam? What a Billion Muslims Really Think*. Born in Egypt but raised most of her childhood in the United States, Mogahed wears a hijab and is a devout Muslim. Before her appointment to the White House Office of Faith-Based and Neighborhood Partnership ended in February 2010, she told an interviewer that her visibility as a Muslim woman in America led to both rewarding experiences and trying ones:

> Like one of any minority, I have experienced prejudice. But much more often I have experienced great gestures of compassion and solidarity from fellow Americans. I'll never forget the first Friday prayer after the 11 September 2001 attacks. Half the congregation were non-Muslims who came to show support at a time when many Muslims were literally afraid even to go to the mosque, for fear of a backlash.[20]

Asra Nomani: A former reporter for the *Wall Street Journal*, Nomani was the main organizer for the 2005 mixed-gender prayer service in New York (see Chapter 8), where Amina Wadud led other Muslims – men and women, all of whom prayed behind her – in what was called the first public service of its kind in modern history. In 2003, Nomani protested against exclusionary policies at her mosque in Morgantown, West Virginia by refusing to pray in the mosque's women-only space, and by posting a tract on the door of her mosque titled, '99 Precepts for Opening Hearts, Minds, and Doors in the Muslim World'. The tract included such tenets as 'reject ignorance, isolation and hatred' and 'chastity and modesty are not the sole measure of a woman's worth.' A single mother, Nomani has continued her activism on a national scale while also continuing to publish journalism and books that explore gender issues in Islam.

Imam Hassan Qazwini: One of America's most prominent Muslim clerics, Qazwini leads the Islamic Center of America in Dearborn, Michigan. The mosque is the largest in the United States, in a state that has the largest concentration of Arab-Americans. Qazwini, who was born and raised in Iraq, is from a long line of Islamic scholars, including his father, Mortada Qazwini, who is the prayer leader at the Shrine of Hussein in Karbala, Iraq. Hassan Qazwini has met frequently with US presidents and, in 2003, opened the session of the US Congress with an invocation that included the words, 'Oh, Allah, endow the people of this great land with a growing trust in one another and an increasing faith in you. Help us all uphold our God-given rights of freedom and equality.'[21] Qazwini has made frequent appearances at interfaith conferences, and wrote a memoir in 2007, *American Crescent: A Muslim Cleric on the Power of his Faith, the Struggle Against Prejudice, and the Future of Islam and America*, that was widely acclaimed. (For my interview with Qazwini, see Chapter 10.)

Feisal Abdul Rauf: In late summer and early fall of 2010, people across the United States knew Rauf's face and his position on the 'Ground Zero mosque': build it as is. Rauf, a liberal Muslim of Egyptian descent who has worked for the US State Department in its effort to establish better understanding between America and the Muslim world, was the main public advocate of the Islamic center proposed for 51 Park Place in lower Manhattan. A practicing Sufi who has led prayer for many years at a Sufi-oriented New York mosque called Masjid al-Farah, Rauf said the proposed Islamic center would be an appropriate symbol of Islam's place in America since the center would be a place for interfaith work and a reminder of Islam's peaceful principles. In 2004, Rauf authored the book, *What's Right with Islam*, whose title was subsequently changed, for the paperback edition, to *What's Right with Islam is What's Right with America*, in which he said that an 'American Islam' is 'bound to evolve that will have a profound impact on Islam in the Muslim world'.[22] The controversy over the Islamic center – and the subsequent debates about whether it belonged so close to the site of the 9/11 attacks – 'helped initiate a discourse that has been very good for the country,'[23] said Rauf, who left the Park51 project in 2011 but is still involved in Islamic advocacy and interfaith work through his own organization, called the Cordoba Initiative.

Zaid Shakir: The co-founder of Zaytuna College, America's first liberal arts college, Shakir is an African-American convert to Islam who spent seven years in Syria studying Islamic law, Quranic studies, and Arabic, graduating from Abu Noor University in Damascus before returning to the United States. In New Haven, Connecticut, he co-founded Masjid al-Islam, which is now known as the New Brunswick Islamic Center, and which he described as the 'most politically active mosque in America'.[24] Among other works, Shakir translated into English *The Heirs of the Prophet*, a fourteenth-century text by Quranic scholar Imam ibn Rajab al-Hanbali that analyzes an important hadith of the Prophet Muhammad. In his 2007 book, *Scattered Pictures: Reflections of an American Muslim*, Shakir talks about the tussle in the United States between different visions of Islam, and his own circuitous path toward a moderate view of the religion, about disposing of the word 'revolution' from his outlook, and about his activist approach to Islam. Shakir has a history of working in the community at both the scholarly level and the street level – in New Haven, for example, he organized night-time groups that would interfere with drug dealers' sales to their clients. Shakir, who has a master's in political science from Rutgers University, frequently speaks around the United States and abroad on issues of Islam and Islamic law. (For excerpts of my interview with Shakir, see Chapter 5 and Chapter 10.)

Azhar Usman: An observant Muslim comedian who is based in Chicago, Usman has made an international name for himself with his stand-up comic routines, which poke fun at Muslims and non-Muslims alike. When I saw him perform in 2004, on his 'Allah Made me Funny' tour with two other Muslim comics, Usman joked about being on a plane and making other passengers nervous because of his long black beard, black clothing and Muslim skull cap. 'Look,' Usman said, as the audience laughed, 'if I'm going to hijack a plane, this isn't the disguise I'm going to go with.'[25] The son of Muslim immigrants from India, Usman graduated from law school at the University of Minnesota before deciding his career was in comedy. Usman has made numerous appearances as an actor, including the 2011 dramatic movie *Mooz-Lum* about American-Muslim life before and after 9/11; he is also a writer of non-fiction works. In 2009, Usman was named as one of the world's 500 most influential Muslims by a joint project administered by the Royal Islamic Strategic Studies Centre in Jordan and Georgetown University's Prince Alwaleed Bin Talal Center for Muslim-Christian Understanding. (For more on Usman, see Chapter 10.)

Amina Wadud: After leading a mixed-gender prayer service in 2005, Wadud continued to spark discussion – in the United States and around the world – about the role of women in Islam, starting with her 2006 book, *Inside the Gender Jihad: Women's Reform in Islam*, which is partly a memoir and partly a scholarly analysis of the way women's roles have been subverted and can be reclaimed. 'Gender justice' is the theme that anchors the book and much of the work of Wadud, an African-American who converted to Islam in 1972 and went on to get her doctorate in Arabic and Islamic studies from the University of Michigan and subsequently study in Egypt at Cairo University and al-Azhar University. Wadud has been a prominent figure in academic circles for 20 years, teaching at the International Islamic University in Malaysia before taking a position at Virginia Commonwealth University, from where she retired in 2008. Wadud's 2005 service led to death threats but also public support, including from Gamal al-Banna, the octogenarian Egyptian scholar who wrote a book saying that women-led prayer services are condoned by Islamic tradition. In his introduction to *Inside the Gender Jihad*, UCLA professor Khaled Abou El Fadl writes that Wadud 'cannot comfortably be fitted with a label such as feminist, progressive, liberal or Islamist'.[26] (For excerpts of my interview with Wadud, see Chapter 8.)

Imam Suhaib Webb: A convert to Islam who is one of America's most popular young imams, Webb grew up in Oklahoma, a state that's part of the US 'Bible belt', where Webb studied Christianity, developed a taste for hip-hop music, and became a DJ and (briefly) a gang member. Webb's conversion to Islam at the age of 20 led him to study with a Senegalese religious scholar for 10 years, then for a further six years at Cairo's al-Azhar University. Fluent in Arabic and a *hafiz* (reciter of the Quran from memory), Webb infuses his talks with references to popular culture, including music and professional sports, and sprinkles his answers with American vernacular, as when he responded to an online question at his website (www. suhaibwebb.com) with, 'Feel me?' (the expression means, 'Do you understand?').[27] Besides his website, which gets more than half a million visitors a month, Webb maintains a Twitter feed (https://twitter.com/ImamSuhaibWebb) that has more than 60,000 followers, and a YouTube channel (https://www. youtube.com/user/SuhaibDWebb) whose videos have been viewed more than 275,000 times. After being named imam in

2011 to the Islamic Society of Boston Cultural Center, which is the largest mosque in the New England area of America, Webb said he represents a new wave of American Muslims – those 'who are born in America, who went overseas to study for a number of years and realize that everything overseas isn't necessarily right. I don't have to be an Arab or a Pakistani to authenticate my Islam.'[28]

Hamza Yusuf: The co-founder of Zaytuna College, Yusuf is a Greek-American convert who has become the United States' leading Muslim intellectual. Labeled 'the Western world's most influential Islamic scholar' by the 2009 publication, *The 500 Most Influential Muslims*,[29] Yusuf studied for 10 years in the Muslim world, including Algeria, Egypt, Mauritania, and Abu Dhabi, where his training included being a muezzin of a mosque. Yusuf first came to attention to many non-Muslim Americans in the days after 9/11, when he was one of a select number of people invited to meet with President George W. Bush. He gave Bush a Quran with passages marked for him to read and told the president that Islam doesn't countenance revenge in response to horrid acts; he warned Bush that the name of the US military's 9/11 response plan, 'Operation Infinite Justice', was offensive to Muslims since 'Infinite Justice' was an attribute of God. (The name was changed to 'Operation Enduring Freedom'.) Through his writings, audio lectures, and talks around the world, Yusuf frequently addresses the place of Islam in the West. In 2010, he was one of four Muslims to co-author, with the Dalai Lama, *Common Ground Between Islam and Buddhism*. Of being Muslim in America, Yusuf has said, 'I would rather live as a Muslim in the West than in most of the Muslim countries, because I think the way Muslims are allowed to live in the West is closer to the Muslim way.'[30]

Rafia Zakaria: A lawyer and writer, Zakaria is the first Muslim woman to serve on the Board of Directors of Amnesty International USA. She founded the Muslim Women's Legal Defense Fund in Indiana, which is co-sponsored by the Muslim Alliance of Indiana – an organization started in the weeks after 9/11. Zakaria grew up in Pakistan before moving to the United States, from where she contributes articles to Pakistani media. Among Zakaria's pieces is one critical of Ayaan Hirsi Ali, the controversial former Dutch member of Parliament who renounced her Muslim faith and, after living in the Netherlands, moved to Washington, DC, where she's a fellow at the American Enterprise Institute. 'While she may be in the U.S. (and now a favorite of certain U.S. conservatives), Hirsi Ali remains distant and seemingly uninterested in the efforts of Muslim-American women to redefine their faith,' Zakaria wrote in reviewing Hirsi Ali's 2010 book, *Nomad: From Islam to America*.[31] 'Her book, while poignantly capturing the weight of structural inequalities crippling Muslim women from Somalia to Pakistan, refuses to take seriously the efforts of Western Muslim women who are refusing to let mullahs define Islam.' Zakaria has said American laws are influencing US Muslim women to rethink the cultural practices of Islam, telling the *New York Times* that, 'If the law [in America] says they are equal, it's hard to see how in their spiritual lives they will accept a whole different identity.'[32]

Mohamed Zakariya: A calligrapher who grew up in Southern California and now lives in the Washington, DC, area, Zakariya designed the first US postage stamp with an Islamic theme – the 'Eid Greetings' stamp that was issued two weeks before the 9/11 attacks. The stamp, which has since been reissued many times, features gold calligraphy that says in Arabic, 'Eid mubarak', which means 'blessed festival'. Zakariya, who converted to

Islam as a teenager, is the only American to have two diplomas from the Research Center for Islamic History, Art and Culture in Istanbul, Turkey. In 2009, when President Barack Obama visited Saudi Arabia, he took with him a gift of calligraphy that he commissioned from Zakariya.

Organizations

Council on American-Islamic Relations: Founded in 1994, the organization advocates on civil rights cases involving Muslims, and sponsors educational and media campaigns related to Islam and Muslims in America. With 28 chapters in 18 states, and with a high media profile, CAIR is one of the largest and most visible Muslim organizations in the United States. Its executive director and co-founder, Nihad Awad, was one of several Muslim Americans who appeared with President George W. Bush on 17 September 2001 at the Islamic Center of Washington, when the president stressed that 'Islam means peace', and that the 9/11 attacks were done by men who abused the precepts of the religion. In 2007, US federal prosecutors named CAIR as an 'unindicted co-conspirator' in a case involving the Holy Land Foundation, a US fund-raising arm that was found to be giving illegal support to Hamas, but in 2010, a US Court of Appeals ruled that the inclusion of CAIR (and other organizations) on the list violated the Fifth Amendment to the Constitution, effectively exonerating CAIR from any connection to the case. In 2011, the organization's chief spokesperson, Ibrahim Hooper – who is a convert to Islam – was named one of the world's most notable Muslims by *The 500 Most Influential Muslims*, an annual work published by the Royal Islamic Strategic Studies Centre in Amman, Jordan.

Islamic Society of North America: One of the largest and oldest Muslim groups in the United States, the society has more than 300,000 members and holds an annual conference near Chicago, Illinois that draws more than 50,000 people – the biggest Muslim gathering in the United States. ISNA also publishes a bi-monthly magazine (*Islamic Horizons*), issues Islamic marriage certificates, certificates of shahadah (the Muslim declaration in one God and Muhammad as his Prophet), and runs youth and adult leadership programs. ISNA is the outgrowth of the Muslim Students Association which was founded in 1963.

Under ISNA's umbrella are a number of other organizations, including the Muslim Students Association and Fiqh Council of North America, a religious body that issues rulings and fatwas on matters of legal importance to American Muslims. In 2010, for example, the council concluded that the US government's electronic airport scanners – which take X-ray-like images of passengers' bodies – infringe Islamic guidelines for modesty, and told Muslim Americans to avoid them and undergo airport 'pat-downs' instead. (See Chapter 4 for more on ISNA and the Muslim Students Association.)

Islamic Supreme Council of America: Started by an American-based Sufi cleric from Lebanon, Sheikh Muhammad Hisham Kabbani, the council holds conferences and classes, gives legal advice, and acts as a moderate voice for Muslims in the United States. Kabbani and the council have clashed with CAIR and ISNA over remarks Kabbani made to the US government in 1999 that implied these organizations were linked with extremism. Kabbani's council emphasizes a Sufi approach of 'building bridges of inter-racial, inter-ethnic and cross-cultural understanding [that] differs from the Wahhabis, who tried to homogenize, standardize and eliminate all variations'.[33] Kabbani has met regularly with Muslim leaders abroad, including the Grand Mufti of Egypt, to discuss issues of confronting extremism. The council claims that, 'for the first time in America' it is integrating 'traditional scholarship with the resolution of contemporary issues affecting the maintenance of Islamic beliefs in a modern, secular society'.[34]

American Islamic Congress: Started in the wake of 9/11 by Muslim-Americans in their twenties and thirties, the congress has become a leading civil rights and activist organization, and promotes what it calls 'progressive' Islam[35] – not just in the United States but in Muslim-majority countries such as Iraq, where it lobbied the government to reserve 25 percent of its jobs for women. The organization frequently integrates with popular culture to connect Muslims with non-Muslims, as in its young persons' essay-writing contest, where judges have included Gloria Steinem and Egyptian-born actor-comic Ahmed Ahmed. Executive director and co-founder Zainab al-Suwaij is from Iraq, where she lived until the failure of the 1991 uprising against Saddam Hussein forced her to leave.

Center for Islamic Pluralism: Co-founded in 2004 by an American-Jewish convert to Islam, Stephen Suleyman Schwartz, who is now executive director, the center has taken a vociferous public stand against what it sees as radical Muslim elements in the United States and abroad. Schwartz, a Sunni Muslim who authored a book that warned about Saudi influence in American mosques (*The Two Faces of Islam: Saudi Fundamentalism and its Role in Terrorism*), has frequently criticized the Council on American-Islamic Relations and the Islamic Society of North America, saying – along with other members of the Center for Islamic Pluralism, including Kemal Silay, a Turkish-born professor at Indiana University – that ISNA was not 'a legitimate representative of mainstream Islamic believers in the West'.[36] ISNA has rejected the accusation, and Schwartz and the center have been criticized for their public belligerence of other Islamic groups.

The Mosque Cares: The organization that Warith Deen Muhammad left behind when he passed away in 2008, The Mosque Cares is one of several American Muslim organizations with an African-American base. It's the only one with Muhammad's imprimatur, which is significant for many American Muslims since he was a product of the Nation of Islam – the son of its longtime leader, Elijah Muhammad – who steered it toward Sunni Islam, away from its unorthodox views. Among the other African-American Muslim organizations is the Nation of Islam. (See Chapters 3, 4, and 6 for more on the Nation of Islam.)

As-Sabiqun: Located in Washington, DC, a 17-minute drive from the White House, As-Sabiqun says Muslim-Americans should adhere to strict Islamic religious beliefs, which the group says take precedence over principles espoused by the Declaration of Independence, the Constitution and other 'man-created covenants' from the United States.[37] As-Sabiqun, which has four branches in California and one in Pennsylvania, believes in establishing an Islamic caliphate. Its imam, Abdul Alim Musa, believes in 'carrying on a direct, face-to-face struggle against the monolithic Zionist American regime',[38] and in having members of his organization follow the writings of such historic Muslim figures as Sayyid Qutb of the Muslim Brotherhood, and Iran's Ayatollah Khomeini.

8 Gender and Religion

How 'Feminist Islam' Has Taken Root and Flourished in America

As a woman muezzin – her hair uncovered – recited the Islamic call to prayer, Amina Wadud knelt on a prayer rug, in front of a congregation of New York City Muslims who were ready to pray in unison behind her. After the muezzin finished the words that have beckoned Muslims to prayer for almost 1,500 years, Wadud stood up and then bowed down toward Mecca. In unison, so did the rows of men and women behind her, who were mixed together without regard to gender. Flashes from cameras recording the event went off in flurries. Scores of video cameras also captured the mixed-gender Friday prayer service – the first one in American history that was led by a woman, and one of the first *jumu'ah* services anywhere where a woman was in charge.

For Wadud, a scholar at Virginia Commonwealth University who had researched Islam for years and has a PhD in Arabic and Islamic studies, that day at the Cathedral of St. John the

Divine in Manhattan – 18 March 2005 – was crucial to show that women have always had the right and the legitimacy to lead Muslim prayer services that are attended by both genders. 'Men and women are both equally essential in creation,' Wadud told the assembled faithful at the cathedral, 'and therefore reciprocally responsible for our relationship with Allah.'[1]

Wadud's message was met with approval by many of those in attendance, but outside the church (which hosted the service after several mosques had declined), police officers guarded the entrances with high-caliber weapons, after reports of death threats against Wadud and other prayer organizers. On the sidewalk, members of a New York political group, Islamic Thinkers Society, protested against the service. 'What does Amina Wadud know about Islam?' one man in the group shouted out.[2] 'What does Amina Wadud know about the Quran and Sunnah? [...] Who the hell is she? Who gave Amina Wadud the authority to speak on behalf of Muslim women?' Next to him stood a protestor with a sign that read: 'Mixed Gender Prayer Today: Hellfire Tomorrow'.[3]

Wadud, the author of *Qur'an and Woman: Rereading the Sacred Text from a Woman's Perspective*, has the support of a phalanx of Muslims, including other Muslim scholars who say that the Quran doesn't prohibit women from delivering Friday prayers – Islam's most important prayers – or leading a mixed-gender service from the front. Wadud's activism has been branded 'Feminist Islam'. Other countries have seen Muslim women questioning policies that limit their involvement in Islamic rituals and typically segregate them into separate prayer areas, but the United States has been an incubator for that kind of scholarly and practical activism – not just through Wadud but a number of others: Asra Nomani, a crusading journalist in West Virginia who had authored what she called the 'Islamic Bill of Rights for Women in the Mosque'; Asma Barlas, director of the Center for the Study of Culture, Race, and Ethnicity at Ithaca College in New York and the author of such books as *Believing Women in Islam: Unreading Patriarchal Interpretations of the Qur'an*; Laleh Bakhtiar, an educational psychologist from Illinois who is the first American woman to translate the Quran into English; Daisy Khan, director of the Women's Islamic Initiative in Spirituality and Equality, a New York-based entity that has members around the world; and Fatima Thompson, a former board director of the California group Muslims for Progressive Values, who has organized several 'pray-ins' at US mosques to protest against rules that force women to pray to the side, at the back or in the basements of Muslim houses of worship.

Verbal and physical confrontations have ensued between Muslim activists and mosque leaders who say the protests of Thompson, Nomani, and others are ill-conceived and ultimately undermine their cause to liberalize Islamic practices. In response, the activists say their approach is grounded in theological precedent and bolstered by America's civil rights history, which has been receptive to scores of other causes (including desegregation and women's empowerment) that have changed entrenched wrongs. Islam isn't the problem, the activists say. It's how the religion has been codified by people in the centuries after the death of the Prophet Muhammad. The Prophet supported women as prayer leaders, they say, but in the centuries after his death, a paternalistic culture interpreted the Quran and the Prophet's hadiths to marginalize women. In the United States, they say, Islam isn't being reinvented – it's being returned to its feminist foundations, in a country where freedom of religion and the constitutional right to expression assure their right to question discriminatory policies.

Wadud, who was born in Maryland to a Methodist minister and a mother descended from African slavery, converted to Islam at the age of 20 in 1972 – a time when activism, particularly among African-Americans, was at its zenith. Islam and the Quran offered Wadud answers that Christianity and Buddhism (which she had previously practiced) did not, and since becoming a devout Muslim, Wadud has maintained her activist zeal.

'The Quran stresses justice, and the African American recognized that under racist laws in America, they were not living the life of justice,' Wadud says in the documentary *The Noble Struggle of Amina Wadud*.[4]

> I was also very strongly conscious of the racial movement because that was the time, just after the '60s, with riots and Malcolm X, and I became interested in: 'Where is my destiny?' I realized that as [a person of] African descent from a slave woman, I had a choice about my body. So I changed my dress. I became a vegetarian. I took care of the fullness of me. And the Quran and learning about Islam opened my mind to a higher level of understanding of relationships between all of the universe and the idea of justice.

For Asra Nomani, justice took on new meaning after the 2002 death of journalist Daniel Pearl, her friend at the *Wall Street Journal* who was kidnapped and beheaded by militants in Pakistan. The people who ordered and carried out Pearl's death were partly inspired by an extremist view of Islam and the Quran, Nomani says. Born in India but raised most of her life in Morgantown, West Virginia, Nomani was with Pearl in Pakistan the day he left for an interview that turned out to be a ruse by kidnappers. After Nomani returned to Morgantown in 2003, she began attending the Islamic Center of Morgantown, where she and other women were required to enter through a back door and to pray in a balcony area with a blocked view of the imam below. In March 2005, after mosque leaders blocked her efforts to change the center's rules for women, Nomani taped on the main entrance a tract titled '99 Precepts for Opening Hearts, Minds, and Doors in the Muslim World', which featured such advice as 'reject ignorance, isolation and hatred'. A mosque member ripped down Nomani's posting minutes after she put it up, but she went on to publish a series of guidelines, one of which was: 'The Islamic Bill of Rights for Women in Mosques', which listed 10 rights, including that women have 'an Islamic right to enter a mosque [...] to enter through the main door [...] to pray in the *musalla* [main prayer area] without being separated by a barrier [...] and to be greeted and addressed cordially.'[5]

Nomani was the main organizer of the mixed-gender prayer service led by Wadud in New York. 'Women's rights should be equal to men's rights,' Nomani told me a few months after the service and the posting of her '99 Precepts'.[6] 'It isn't Islamically required that women be separated and segregated. It's like we're in the early stages of the civil rights movement, trying to build up public pressure and embarrass these mosques when they treat you like a pariah.'

Pressure has been applied by different waves of women, including Fatima Thompson, whom Nomani has compared to Rosa Parks, the African-American woman who, in 1955, refused to relinquish her seat at the front of a segregated bus in the southern state of Alabama. Parks' historic defiance helped set the tone for America's civil rights movement. Thompson's defiance in 2010, where she refused to leave her place of prayer in the musalla at the Islamic Center of Washington, set off volleys of admonition from the center's officials, including a woman administrator telling Thompson and her cohorts to go to the back of the mosque. 'If you want to come here to pray,' the administrator said, 'you can pray. But you cannot come here and disrespect the mosque.'[7] After the police were called in, Thompson left and prayed outside, rather than in what she and others have called the 'penalty box' – the prayer area for women that is cordoned off by barriers and screens.

Nomani, Thompson, and other Muslim women have borrowed techniques and language from earlier periods of American activism. In the 1960s, for example, protestors held 'sit-ins' – demonstrations where they'd refuse to move from their positions on the ground – to disrupt gatherings or draw attention to their cause. In 2010, Thompson helped organized 'pray-ins', where Muslim women would refuse to budge from their places in the mosque. Nomani has called the practice of separating men and women in mosques 'gender apartheid'.[8] At Islam's holiest mosque, Masjid al-Haram in Mecca, men and women pray together during the hajj, the pilgrimage that is one of Islam's five pillars, points out Nomani, who has completed the hajj.

For Muslim feminists, America is paradoxical – a country where, more than anywhere else in the world, they can challenge their role in Islam and the mosque, but where mosque life is still restrictive, even after years of highly visible protests. Almost a third of American mosques (31 percent) prohibit women from serving on the governing or executive board,[9] and almost two-thirds of mosques (66 percent) require women to pray behind a curtain or partition in a different room from the main prayer area,[10] according to a 2001 survey by the Council on American-Islamic Relations, a prominent civil liberties organization based in Washington, DC. The trend has been for greater gender segregation, not less – in 1994, fewer US mosques (52 percent) forced women to pray in isolated spots, according to CAIR.[11]

In 2005, the organization Women in Islam, Inc., which is based in New York, and the Arizona-based Islamic Social Services Association, published a 15-page booklet that argued for more inclusiveness in American mosques. *Women Friendly Mosques and Community Centers: Working Together to Reclaim our Heritage*[12] cited Sunnah, hadiths, and Islamic scholarship to persuade US (and Canadian) mosques to change their policies on where women pray, what entrances they use, and what leadership positions they can occupy. Labeled 'an urgent need for action',[13] the booklet – supported by CAIR, the Islamic Society of North America, and other US Muslim organizations – said that the mosques' most important sermon, the Friday *khutba*, should be more mindful of words that demean women. The booklet stated,

> Women perceive that the khutba must become more sensitive to the language and culture of North America and are not balanced in their content. Gender issues, when addressed in the khutba, must be discussed in ways that highlight the differences between culture and religion and recognize the diversity of Muslim women's experiences.[14]

Laleh Bakhtiar was mindful of language and the distinction between culture and religion when she issued a new English translation of the Quran in 2007. A practicing Muslim in Chicago who had spent 20 years living in Iran, Bakhtiar explained that she wanted to eliminate loaded words that, in many previous Quranic translations, had been mistakenly used to condone violence. The most controversial passage in *The Sublime Quran* is surah 4:34, which dictates how men should treat wives who are disobedient. In standard English translations, the passage – based on the original Arabic root word, *daraba* – usually allows men to hit their wives, if only 'lightly'. In her years researching translations and classical Arabic, Bakhtiar found that *daraba* had more than 25 meanings, including 'beat' but also 'go away'. The Prophet Muhammad never struck women, and other passages in the Quran – particularly surah 2:231, which disallows physical force against wives – make clear that misogyny is forbidden. After consulting with other scholars, Bakhtiar reworked surah 4:34 to say that men who are at a serious standstill with their wives should simply 'go away' from them, not retaliate with physical force. Though other scholars had previously voiced the same ideas in lectures, *The Sublime Quran* was the first printed translation to feature the reworking of 'go away', Bakhtiar says.

Within days of publication, *The Sublime Quran* prompted heated debate between those who said Bakhtiar had no right to contravene traditional translations and those who said she was part of a tradition within Islam of correcting religious misunderstandings. Among those who came to Bakhtiar's defense was Hadia Mubarak, a daughter of Syrian immigrants who was raised in Florida and became the first woman president of the Muslim Students Association. Speaking to the online publication Beliefnet, Mubarak said that Muslim scholars had debated surah 4:34 from almost the beginning of Islam, and that many foremost interpreters would have agreed with Bakhtiar's translation. Mubarak continued:

> In my own research, I found discussion of that verse has gone on for a very long time, as far back as the scholar Ibn Abbas [who was 13 when the Prophet Muhammad died], who was a successor to the companions of the Prophet. He said in his *tafsir* [interpretation of the Quran] that his fellow scholars misunderstood the verse. He understood that phrase *wadribuhunna* [*daraba* in root form] to be in an imperative form that actually means God is saying, 'Don't beat them'.[15]

The Sublime Quran makes changes throughout the holy book. Instead of referring to 'Allah', *The Sublime Quran* always uses the word 'God'. And instead of using the word 'infidel' to mean those who have fallen from the faith of Islam, Bakhtiar uses the phrasing 'ungrateful', as in people 'who are ungrateful' for the wisdom of God. *The Sublime Quran* emphasizes inclusivity, not exclusivity, Bakhtiar says. The book could not have been published in a Muslim-majority country, Bakhtiar told me:

> They would never have allowed this to go to print. In America, the freedom of speech, the freedom of religion, the open society – all of these are reasons why the women's movement was able to be active here and then try to influence other areas of the world. If you live in the Muslim world, it's very difficult. This would have not have been published.
>
> Surah 4:31, with the words 'go away' instead of 'beat,' has never been part of a (previous) translation for the Quran. I felt very strongly it had to be, to have an impact – to move forward on this issue, so it's not that God sanctions a husband to beat his wife in the name of God.

On the subject of how welcoming mosques are to women, Bakhtiar says she has stopped attending mosques altogether, preferring to pray at home instead. She says she is one in a long line of people – men and women – who have embraced (in Arabic *futwwah* and in Persian *javanmardi*) the tradition of Islamic outspokenness and spiritual questioning. After publishing *The Sublime Quran*, Bakhtiar met men who supported her work and women who discounted it, making her realize how complex the issue is. 'I've spoken to many men who agree with the interpretation, "Go away". And I've also spoken with many women who think [based on surah 4:31] that women should be beaten [in extreme cases],' Bakhtiar says.

> So I realize it's not a woman or feminist issue – it's more a human rights issue. And women – particularly those educated in the Middle East – they usually follow what the men have said. That's called imitation. But the cultural ambience is so overwhelming and overpowering in those countries that you end up thinking just like a man would think.

Bakhtiar, who is an active member of the Women's Islamic Initiative in Spirituality and Equality, says she 'feels very blessed to be in this country'. She doesn't wear a hijab. She says it is a 'woman's choice' whether to cover her hair. Wadud says it is a mistake to confuse a Muslim woman's faith with the way she dresses. Both women dress modestly, and Wadud always has on a hijab in public – as she did at the mixed-gender prayer session at the Cathedral of St. John the Divine in Manhattan – and wore the *niqab* (full face veil) for four years. But Wadud says she is now 'flexible' with her outlook on Islamic dress. 'In more formal settings, I keep the hijab [on],' she told documentarian Elli Safari.[16] 'But if I cut the grass or go to a gym, I don't wear anything on my hair.'

'Allah did not say, "I'm sorry you don't have a hijab, so I cannot accept your prayer,"' she told Safari, before taking off her Muslim headscarf for the camera.

> That's not how Allah would look at a human being. Because Allah already sees all the way through – not through our clothes only, but through our hearts [...] God has the capacity to listen and to respond just as much to [a woman without a hijab] or a woman on the street who was in prostitution because it's the only way she can make a income to provide for her family. Or

a woman who doesn't want to pray all the time but still believes in God. That none of these women are any better than another woman, just as no men are better than a woman [...] Allah's decision are based on the *nafs* [soul]; is your heart really true to Islam or is it just an idea that you flourishly show off to the people. All religions have symbols. But the symbols only have meanings the people have embedded in that meaning. And the symbols aren't the real thing; the real thing can only be between the heart, the actions and obedience to Allah. And Allah accepts only the full picture. If you have a hijab and you are a hypocrite, Allah recognizes that. If you don't have a hijab, and you are sincere, Allah recognizes equally. And there's no problem with Allah's vision. She can see.

Wadud's reference to God as 'she' would be deemed heretical by many Muslims, but the reference is supported by Quranic scholarship, argue Muslim scholars. The Quran says that God is above all creatures and creation – it doesn't assign a gender to God, says Asma Barlas,[17] the New York professor who was raised in Pakistan before moving to the United States, where she authored *Believing Women in Islam: Unreading Patriarchal Interpretations of the Qur'an*. Barlas told Dutch philosopher Fons Elders, for a documentary produced by Dutch Islamic Broadcast,[18] that the Quran is open to more accurate English and Arabic translations by Islamic scholars – men and women. Misogyny, Barlas says, has no place in Islam, whether it's practiced in the United States or a Muslim-majority country.

'Like every other text in the world, the Quran also is also open to multiple readings,' Barlas told Elders.[19]

We ought not to [...] make it seem that there's a natural connection between the Quran and women's oppression [...]

The Quran is not a feminist text, but what I do argue is that the Quran provides a certain framework – epistemological, ontological framework – within which we can theorize radical, sexual equality. Basically meaning, that if the Quran teaches that women and men are ontologically from the same self, the same nafs, it completely changes the way in which Muslims in particularly are used to thinking that women as having a secondary stage. That she was taken from the man's ribs – there is no such narrative in the Quran. And more importantly for me, the fact that the Quran doesn't masculinize God, doesn't engender God, doesn't patriarchalize God – in other words, we are told that God is uncreated and unlike anything, so God is beyond sex and gender [...] I call it an anti-patriarchal view of God. If God cannot be patriarchalized, then I feel like the Quran, which is God's speech, also should not be patriarchalized.

More than one person has said that Asma Barlas, Amina Wadud, and other Muslim scholars deemed feminists 'could blossom only in the West'. Even if that's true, their scholarship and their actions are noted around the world, including Muslim-majority countries. The prayer service that Wadud led in 2005 was commented on by imams and devout Muslims everywhere. In many circles, Wadud was called an apostate and worse.

In contrast, one of her supporters, Mona Eltahawy – an Egyptian-born commentator who lives in New York – after praying behind Wadud, came home to find a correspondence from a man in Saudi Arabia. 'At least now,' the man wrote to Eltahawy, 'I know that my children (if I ever have any) will see a religion with more equality.'[20]

It is that kind of response that American Muslim feminists are trying to engender. Even 15 centuries after the birth of Islam, they say that the religion's practices can be reimagined.

The United States is the ideal place from which to do that. The country has become a kind of nationwide think tank that lets them share ideas with each other and with strangers who are free to disagree and offer a countervailing view. Still, Wadud told me in an interview, these ideas shouldn't be reduced to the category of 'feminism' or even 'American Islam'. What she is doing with her activism, and books like *Inside the Gender Jihad: Women's Reform in Islam*, is to show that the practice of Islam has been co-opted by people who may not even realize their mistaken ways. The landmark mixed-gender service at the Cathedral of St. John the Divine in 2005 was preceded by more than three decades of other work – from public forums to private scholarship – that convinced Wadud of its need.

Muslim men have encouraged Wadud. She tells me:

I've had more than 35 years of study of Islam. In 1994, I was invited to a conference, and subsequently to a two-week lecture tour, in South Africa. When I was there for the conference, some of the progressive brothers who had also been participants in the apartheid struggles discussed with me the possibility of what we now say is the gender jihad. That included an explicit invitation to give the khutba for a Friday service in a mosque in South Africa. This was a new idea for me then. But it was not an idea that I had any misgivings about until the results of participating in the Friday prayer led to so much backlash. And in the face of the backlash, what I decided I needed to do more than anything else was to understand what my perspective was on the issue and why, and so from that point on, although I have been asked on a number of occasions to lead a mixed-gender prayer, I refused categorically in every situation. And in 2004, I was invited to become an advisor to a fledgling organization, the Progressive Muslim Network, that never really got a chance to get beyond the fledglingness because of controversy that also arose. With that invitation was also information about the planning for a conference that would be organized at Harvard University Divinity School, and they said they wanted to start on Friday, and they invited me to do the khutba and the prayer service. And my position had changed to the point where I had answers. And the answers were sufficient to me to ascertain my own intention relative to the level of controversy of such a thing. So I agreed.

But this planned service never happened. As Wadud recounts,

the conference – first of all because of the problems in getting the fledgling organization off the ground with the conflicts that came up regarding it – did not go on. Nevertheless, the seeds for the idea of having a public mixed-gender prayer led by a woman were already out there, and it did not die. However, logistically there were a lot of things that needed to be put in place for it to really happen. And nobody had control of those logistics if I was going to participate, because I lived at the time in Virginia. And nobody was coming to Virginia to do it. So how was this going to be taken care of? It happened, coincidentally, that I was invited to Auburn Theological Seminary [in New York] to give a discussion and the topic was basically gender, God, and Islam, and at the time, Asra Nomani asked me if I would do the prayer in New York and stay after my time at Auburn Seminary. So my participation is welded to my own research and conclusions with regard to the manner of prayer in Islam.

After the prayer service in New York, Wadud published *Inside the Gender Jihad*, which argues that, soon after the Prophet Muhammad's death, women were mostly kept from participating in Islam's 'paradigmatic foundations', and that centuries of exclusion have taken a toll. 'Not only did men, men's experiences of the world – including their experiences with women – and men's ideas and imagination determine how Islam is defined for themselves,' Wadud writes, 'they also defined Islam for women. Men have proposed what it means to be Muslim on the presumption that the male experience is normative, essential, and universal to all humankind.'[21]

Wadud says her outspokenness has led to 'consequences' that have ostracized her from more conservative Islamic centers. Death threats have occurred. Nomani, Bakhtiar, and other reform-minded men and women have also experienced retribution. Wadud says the 2005 prayer service was important to show that Islamic practices do not have to be frozen in time. 'I don't see Islam as a dead religion,' she told me.

I see it as alive and dynamic. So when people say that I tended to 'change tradition' by leading the prayer, I say instead that as we believe in Allah, we live Islam. So we are part of the *living* traditions of Islam. And this [her prayer service] is as much a part of living Islam as anything else, and living it within the context of a very different understanding of gender, of gender roles, of gender identity, and how all of those different understandings affect how we even participate in Islam today. We don't leave gender out of the formula. But there were obviously periods of time in Islamic history where, yes, there were women and men – but 'gender' as a category of thought, and as a structure in society? That wasn't part of the way people thought. So do we stop thinking about it?

No, says Wadud. A thousand times no.

9 In Politics, Muslim-Americans Progress One Step at a Time

In the state of Texas, southwest of downtown Houston between George Bush Park (named after George H.W. Bush, not his son) and a trio of golf clubs, lie a series of distinct neighborhoods that make up 'District F'. The district may be Houston's most diverse, with large percentages of Hispanic, black, and white residents, along with a growing number of residents who are Pacific Islander, Native American, Indian, Pakistani, Chinese, and other ethnicities. When people talk of the 'American melting pot', they might as well be referring to Houston's District F – and to Masrur Javed Khan, a.k.a. 'M.J.' Khan, the Pakistani-American who represented District F on the Houston City Council for three consecutive terms, from 2003 to 2009.

Khan was the first Muslim and the first Pakistani-American to be elected to the council, one of the first Muslims to win any elected office in Texas, and the first Pakistani-American to win a notable position in a major American city. His historic victory was covered closely by the media in Pakistan, from where he had immigrated in 1976. Pakistani-American groups heralded Khan's victory, as did Muslim-American groups. Khan's opponent in the 2003 race, Terry McConn, suggested that Khan would step into office with a pro-Muslim agenda. 'Mr. Khan tells Muslims, "We as Muslims must defeat the white Christian,"' McConn told the *Dallas Morning News* in the days before the 2003 election.[1] 'It's a scary situation.'

Khan didn't scare anyone during his three terms on the Houston City Council, which were marked mainly by 'bread and butter' issues, like fixing streets, reducing crime, and allocating district monies. Few Muslims live in District F (though as many as 100,000 Pakistani-Americans live in the greater Houston area[2]). Essentially, Khan was a 'happen-to-be' Muslim – an engineer and real estate developer who showcased his religion during the campaign trail but didn't make it an issue there or in office. People in Houston's District F voted for Khan without fixating on his religion.

'There are virtually no Muslims in that district,' Khan tells me. 'Most Americans will vote for someone they think will be the best person to represent them, regardless of race, religion, color or any other orientation. Houston is one of the most diverse cities in the country. I always say what Houston is like is what America will be in a few decades, if not sooner.'

Khan's experience in politics mirrors that of America's best-known Muslim politician: Keith Ellison, who became the first elected Muslim member of the US Congress in 2007. Ellison, an African-American who converted to Islam in 1982, was voted in from one of Minnesota's most diverse districts – District 5, historically Democratic, is the state's most urban area (incorporating the city of Minneapolis), and where 18 percent of households speak a language other than English at home.[3] Like Khan, Ellison had a lot of civic experience on his curriculum vitae before running for Congress, and like Khan,

Ellison's religion was called into question by opponents, but was ultimately a non-factor in the election – as it has been in his tenure as a congressman. Another Muslim member of Congress was elected in 2008, when Andre Carson, an African-American convert, was voted in from the state of Indiana. Carson's district, which includes the capital, Indianapolis, is – like Houston's District F and Minnesota's District 5 – a heavily diverse one. Thirty percent of the district's residents are African-American.[4]

At the state level since 9/11, seven Muslims have been elected to Senate seats or similar positions, and about 20 Muslims have attained positions (like Khan) on city council or other local seats, according to the American Muslim Taskforce on Civil Rights and Elections, an advocacy group. In 2010, about 30 Muslims were serving in elected US offices that gave them widespread responsibility over civic matters. 'It's very small,' Agha Saeed, national chairman of the American Muslim Taskforce, tells me, 'but it's an important [development] in the last 10 years.' In 2000, few Muslim candidates ran for office, says Saeed, a University of California lecturer who immigrated to the United States from Pakistan. 'The word "Muslim" was enough to disqualify them,' Saeed says. By 2010, hundreds of Muslim-Americans, with the encouragement of the American Muslim Taskforce and other organizations, had campaigned for office. Among them was Ferial Masry, a high-school teacher who in 2004 ran for the California Assembly and became the first Saudi-American in US history to vie for elected office. Masry, whose eldest son was a US solider in Iraq, lost her race and ran again for the California Assembly in 2010, only to be defeated again – but her continuing campaigns, and those of M.J. Khan (who lost a 2009 race for Houston City controller), Ellison (who was re-elected in 2010 and 2012), and others have inspired a new wave of Muslim-Americans to seek higher office. Among aspiring politicians and long-time activists, there is even talk of having a Muslim-American president in the White House – perhaps in the next decade. Whether this is wishful thinking or the calculations of political realists depends on your perspective. Among US religious groups, Muslim-Americans are the least likely to cast a ballot: just 64 percent are registered to vote, compared to 90 percent for Jewish-Americans, 90 percent for Protestant-Americans, 76 percent for Catholic-Americans, and 81 percent for the general population, according to the Gallup Center for Muslim Studies.[5]

'Many of the Muslims who came to this country came from countries where voting was a dangerous and dirty thing to do,' Mukit Hossain, executive director of the Muslim American Political Action Committee, told the *Washington Post* in 2006.[6] 'We have to convince them that voting is not only safe and clean but it is a civic responsibility.'

Because the total number of US Muslims is disputed, it's unclear how many American Muslims vote, but the American Muslim Taskforce estimates that 4 million Muslims were registered for the 2008 presidential election, when 89 percent of Muslims went for Barack Obama, its polling suggests.[7] One of Obama's first appointees was Dalia Mogahed, the hijab-wearing executive director of the Gallup Center for Muslim Studies, who was named a White House advisor on Muslim affairs. But how much clout do Muslim-Americans have with the Obama administration? Saeed says that FBI harassment of US Muslims has increased under Obama, and that a 'guilt-by-association' political harassment of American Muslims has also worsened, indicated by the 'Ground Zero mosque' controversy, when many conservative politicians, including Republican congressman Peter King of New York, came out forcefully against the proposed Islamic center in lower Manhattan. 'It is insensitive and uncaring for the Muslim community to build a mosque in the shadow of Ground Zero,' said King,[8] who as head of the House Committee on Homeland Security held hearings in 2011 on what he calls 'the radicalization of the American Muslim community'. Though Obama has spoken out in favor of the Park51 Islamic Center, 'every indicator for Muslims has been worse under this administration,' Saeed tells me, saying that he is worried about a new 'McCarthyite, anti-Communist-style mindset' against Muslim-Americans.

Despite his high profile, Ellison has been selective on issues relating specifically to Muslim-Americans. His advisors told him to stay away from the charged debate over the Park51 Islamic Center, but Ellison resisted the political temptation to remain quiet, and said that opposition to the center was being fomented by anti-Obama groups and those who despised Muslims: 'The real drivers of it are people who openly proclaim that Barack Obama is not a citizen. The real organizers of this thing are people who are just proponents of religious bigotry. Nothing more, nothing less.'[9] Still, Ellison qualified his comments to the *Star Tribune* newspaper in Minnesota, saying his feelings weren't a product of his Muslim faith but the United States' emphasis on freedom of religion. 'My advocacy on this question is not rooted in my own religious beliefs,' he told the paper.[10] 'If this were happening to some Jews, or some Christians, or some Baha'i people, I would be saying they can build their temple where they please, where they have a legal right to do so.'

Politically, Muslim-American politicians walk a proverbial fine line: speak out too much about Islam and Muslim-Americans, and they risk alienating their constituents; speak out too little, and they risk alienating Muslim-Americans who expect them to make a bigger difference. In December 2008, when Ellison undertook the hajj to Mecca, he didn't announce it in public, and when he returned, he said the trip was 'transformative'[11] but completely unrelated to his duties as a congressman, explaining: 'We weren't really trying to turn this into a political thing. This is just me trying to be the best person I can be [...] It really didn't have anything to do with me being a congressman.'[12]

Though Ellison has tried to distance his political life from his religious life, the two frequently overlap. Even his pilgrimage to Mecca became politicized when it emerged that the Muslim American Society of Minnesota paid for the trip. In 2009, the American Civil Liberties Union (ACLU) sued the society for allegedly having teachers at its Minnesota charter school, the Tarek ibn Ziyad Academy, advocate Islam. Through the society, the school was the indirect recipient of government funding – almost $900,000 in 2006 and 2007 – so the alleged advocacy was in violation of federal guidelines that prohibit public institutions from promoting religion.[13] Ellison was thus linked to an institution that its critics say is among those 'secretly' planning to impose Islam on America. The Muslim American Society of Minnesota denied the ACLU's charges.

The Tarek ibn Ziyad Academy – whose student body comprised immigrant children, many Somali-American – excelled in statewide testing, prompting other schools to copy its teaching methods, which included having students use fingers as a tactile way to remember analytical techniques. Still, in the summer of 2011, the academy was forced to close after the state of Minnesota – reacting to the ACLA lawsuit – rejected the school's request for a new academic and financial overseer. The academy was co-founded by Asad Zaman, a Bangladeshi-American who was its principal and is one of the Minneapolis area's best-known Muslims – on a par with Ellison, who is his friend. In fact, Zaman accompanied Ellison on the hajj in 2008, and Zaman himself has steadily become much more political: in

2004, he was a delegate to the Democratic National Convention in Boston – one of about 40 Muslim-American delegates – and, like others there, he said he got more involved in politics because of the perceived anti-Muslim bias among elected leaders.

'I am an American by choice,' Zaman said then.[14] 'I chose an America that would guarantee my freedom, and an America that would guarantee my rights. This [scapegoating of Muslims] is sad. This is not the America we wanted it to be.'

Another Muslim delegate at the convention, Massachusetts software developer Parwez Wahid, put it more diplomatically: 'We're trying to become mainstream. If Muslims want a greater influence, then there's a role they have to play in American politics.'[15]

That role doesn't have to be as an elected official. Many Muslim organizations – including the Council on American-Islamic Relations, the Islamic Society of North America, the American Islamic Congress, the Islamic Supreme Council of America, and the American Muslim Taskforce on Civil Rights and Elections – lobby elected officials. Saeed met with George W. Bush many times during his two terms in the White House, asking him to repeal laws that allowed for greater scrutiny of suspected criminals, and asking him to appoint a qualified Muslim-American to a prominent position to broaden Bush's Cabinet. Bush never did. Obama never visited a mosque during his 2007–8 campaign for the presidency, and during a campaign stop in Detroit, Obama volunteers prohibited two Muslim women, Hebba Aref and Shimaa Abdelfadeel, from being on the podium behind the then-senator because they feared the women's hijabs would send the wrong message to people looking on from the audience – or at home on television. Aref's friend, Ali Kousson, told *Politico*, a news outlet, that the volunteer 'explained to me that because of the political climate and what's going on in the world and what's going on with Muslim Americans it's not good for her to be seen on TV or associated with Obama.'[16] Obama subsequently apologized for the actions, and once he was elected president, he talked to the media – and the world – about his father's Muslim religion, and his connections to Islam, but those links were downplayed for the campaign, when he denied (vociferously) that he was a Muslim and stressed (and re-stressed) his Christian beliefs and church-going. For Muslim-Americans, the most poignant moment of the campaign took place on television in the weeks before the election when Colin Powell – a retired four-star general, Secretary of State under George W. Bush, and a staunch supporter of Republican candidates – endorsed Obama and scolded Obama's critics for trying to impugn the senator's character by suggesting he was Muslim. So what if Obama were a Muslim? Powell said,

> I'm also troubled by, not what Senator McCain says, but what members of the party say. And it is permitted to be said such things as, 'Well, you know that Mr. Obama is a Muslim.' Well, the correct answer is, he is not a Muslim, he's a Christian. He's always been a Christian. But the really right answer is, what if he is? Is there something wrong with being a Muslim in this country? The answer's no, that's not America. Is there something wrong with some seven-year-old Muslim-American kid believing that he or she could be president? Yet, I have heard senior members of my own party drop the suggestion, 'He's a Muslim and he might be associated with terrorists.' This is not the way we should be doing it in America.[17]

Ellison, though, has cautioned Muslim-American candidates against trumpeting their faith in campaigns, telling the *Washington Post* on the ninth anniversary of 9/11, 'Muslim candidates lose when they try to run as a Muslim, which, of course, is fair. Christians don't vote for people just because they're Christian. Jews don't vote for people just because they're Jews. They want to know: "What are you going to do for me and my family?"[18]

That's what M.J. Khan discovered in Houston. Born and raised in Pakistan, Khan – who moved to the United States to attend college – still speaks with a Pakistani accent. In beating McConn for his first term on the Houston City Council, Khan defeated a white attorney who had made a name for himself by coaching a Houston-area kids' baseball team to the Little League World Series in 2000. Little League is a quintessential American sport, and McConn – the son of Houston's former mayor, Jim McConn – was a favorite to win the District F job since his name had more cachet than Khan's. Another factor: the incumbent office-holder was McConn's brother-in-law, who put his support behind McConn. Another factor is that in previous races, white turnout accounted for the majority of the district's vote.[19] But the year Khan was elected proved to be a watershed year in Houston – the year when a candidate of color was voted in by people who were white and, because of increased turnout, people who were non-white.[20] Hispanics are the largest ethnic group in District F, representing about 40 percent of the population,[21] but 'there was very little voting from them even though they were the largest group in the district,' Khan says. 'That seat had been held (for years) by Anglo, white conservative Christians.'

Before running for the seat, Khan held a number of civic positions in Houston that, he says, prepared him for the city council – and prepared voters to accept him as a bona fide candidate. Khan's previous positions included: advisory director for the Houston West Chamber of Commerce; board member of the Holocaust Museum Houston; president of the Pakistani-American Association of Greater Houston; vice president of the Islamic Society of Greater Houston; member of the Small Business Advisory Board of the Texas Natural Resource Conservation Commission. 'I was not', he says, 'a total stranger.' Especially after knocking on at least 4,000 doors in the district during the campaign, which went from November 2002 to November 2003. The campaigning started a year after 9/11.

'The other council members, and people who took an interest in the race wrote me off,' Khan says.

> Many of them told me, 'What are you doing? You're wasting your time. You're not a blue-eyed boy. Don't do it.' [...] I have a different name. A different religion. A different culture. A different look. But I think that's the best thing about America – that people who are like me can aspire to public office, and can succeed [...] Two or three households (out of 4,000 that I personally had dealings with in the campaign) asked me about my religion, but by and large, people didn't care. My opponent tried to make it an issue, but politics is a strange thing.

The strangeness of politics means that what is true in one part of the United States may not be true in another. In the summer of 2010 in Dallas County, Alabama – which is 63 percent African-American and 36 percent white – the incumbent state senator, an African-American Muslim, Yusuf Abdus-Salaam, lost his seat in the Democratic primary to a white Christian, Darro Melton. Abdus-Salaam is an imam; Melton is a pastor. Abdus-Salaam, a four-term senator and the first Muslim-American to serve in the Alabama legislature, lost by less than 500 votes. 'There's nothing to explain my defeat other than religion,' Abdus-Salaam told a reporter.[22]

Even in the liberal San Francisco Bay area, there is a perception that Muslims need to be cautious. In the fall of 2001, when lawyer Maad Abu-Ghazalah decided to run for a congressional seat against Tom Lantos, Abu-Ghazalah's friend advised him to eliminate 'Abu' from his name during the political campaign. Born in the Palestinian territories and raised in Saudi Arabia, Abu-Ghazalah rejected the suggestion.

Khan says Muslim-Americans – at least in the first part of the twenty-first century – have to be conscious of how their religion affects voters and their own place if they obtain office. 'One thing I always say when I go and talk to young people,' says Khan, 60,

> is that everybody's religion is really important to them, and yours should be too. You should take a lot of pride in what you believe in – otherwise don't believe in it. But when you are out there serving the public, you cannot be the champion of your religion. Otherwise, someone else will be the champion of their religion, and that may conflict with you. Yes, take your learning and teaching from your religion, because all religions teach good, and practice that, but instead of being 'the Muslim council member for the Muslims', be the best council member who happens to be a Muslim, and because of that upbringing and faith, these are the good things you are doing for everybody. That's what I tried to practice. I didn't push anything because I was a Muslim only for Muslims. All the things that are good for the community are good for the Muslims, also.

The only time that Khan's religion became a factor during his council terms was when Houston was competing for state funds geared toward local businesses, and the city was advocating for a brewery. Khan recused himself from the vote since his faith prohibits the consumption (and, in effect, the promotion) of alcohol.

Out of office, Khan is mulling his future. He says he might run for office again. For the vast majority of Muslim-Americans, seeking office isn't a viable option. They don't want to endure the long campaigning that's required, or the raising of money that's needed to sustain a candidacy. Voting, however, is free. And Muslim-Americans are more aware than ever that paying attention to issues – not just during election cycles but year-round – is as big a part of politics as picking a candidate who might be the next president of the United States.

10 Conflicts and Co-Existence

The American Dream in the Twenty-First Century

Standing at the main pulpit of Michigan's Islamic Center of America, Imam Hassan Qazwini surveys the large crowd of worshipers who are sitting on the carpet before him. With his black turban signifying his descent from the Prophet Muhammad, his dark brown cloak identifying him as a Shiite cleric, and with a voice that is tinged with the Iraqi Arabic accent of his childhood, Qazwini begins the second part of his khutbah – the most important sermon of the week for religious Muslims. Qazwini speaks without notes in a matter-of-fact way, never resorting to yelling or finger-pointing or any kind of wild gesticulating, even though it is clear that he is agitated.

A week earlier, the Texas State Board of Education passed a resolution that warned about 'pro-Islamic/anti-Christian bias' in Texas social studies textbooks.[1] The board's resolution cited three instances of what it said was blatant bias, including one book that gave

82 student text lines to Christian beliefs, practices, and holy writings but 159 (almost twice as many) to those of Islam; describing Crusaders' massacres of European Jews yet ignoring the Muslim Tamerlane's massacre of perhaps 90,000 co-religionists at Baghdad in 1401, and of perhaps 100,000 Indian POWs at Delhi in 1398; thrice charging medieval Christians with sexism; and saying the Church 'laid the foundations for anti-Semitism'.[2]

Passed on 24 September 2010, the resolution was non-binding, but it sent a warning to publishers of US school textbooks: rework what you say about Islam or your tomes won't be sold in one of America's biggest textbook markets. Qazwini tells his mosque's adherents that the school board's pronouncement sets a dangerous precedent for Islam in the United States.

'The state of Texas made a very troubling decision, a very unwise decision,' he says, noting that the board's passage came at a time of the 'Ground Zero mosque' controversy and other news events that put American Muslims on the defensive.[3]

What's really alarming, my dear brothers and sisters, is that this could be a contagious process. You will not be surprised if you probably hear tomorrow that Oklahoma's board of education will be doing the same. Florida's board of education will be doing the same. And there are another [47] states that may follow suit and do the same thing. That's not fair. We Muslims need to speak up, my brothers and sisters.

Qazwini practices what he preaches, but he's also in a unique position – someone who has the ear of US presidents and other elected leaders; someone who can interpret current events through the dual prisms of Islam and American politics; someone who's invited into synagogues and churches to explain a religion that puzzles – if not reviles – many Americans. A few months after his khutbah talk about the Texas State Board of Education's resolution, Qazwini tells me that Muslims in America face challenges and opportunities that are different from those faced by Muslims in the Middle East, and that Islam is developing on a different track in America. The differences are subtle but profound.

'When we talk about Islam, there are the main principles that do not vary from one society to another,' Qazwini tells me.

And there are issues pertaining to the society that you live in, and these are the variables that we see in any religion, including Islam. So, for example, when Islam speaks about hijab, the Islamic dress code for women, the concept of hijab is the same but the application of hijab may vary from one country to another. Muslims living in the United States have their own distinct practice that has a particular color or shade that is shaped by the American society. Again, that does not mean we are inventing another religion. Rather, the application of Islam here could differ a little bit from the one that is in, say, Iraq.

Take the issue of the hijab. In Iraq, the hijab is an integral part of religious women's lives, but in the United States, the head garment is optional for many women. In a major 2007 survey of American Muslims by the Pew Research Center, nearly half of those responding (48 percent) said they never wore hijabs, with 8 percent saying they wore the headscarf 'only some of the time'.[4] Mosque treatment of women is also different in America than in the greater Muslim world. Most mosques in Iraq, for example, require men and women to pray in completely different spaces, says Qazwini. The Islamic Center of America has women pray behind men, but in the same hall. In a 2001 survey, *The Mosque in America: A National Portrait*, published by the Council on American-Islamic Relations, almost two-thirds of US mosques (66 percent) had women pray behind a curtain or partition or in another room.[5]

'If you go to the Middle East, into Iraq or Iran, most mosques separate and segregate men and women,' Qazwini tells me.

Here in the United States, in our mosque, many women are separated but they're not segregated. They pray in the same hall, but men pray in the front and women in the back section of the mosque. This is not something we have invented. Rather, this remains within the general understanding of Islam itself. In some conservative societies, they do not tolerate men and women being in one hall – they insist on segregation. In our mosque, being the United States, we don't see that segregation is a must. Rather, it is mostly something that the culture of the indigenous nations in the Middle East have a lot to do with. And we know that, often, faith and culture – they overlap.

It is the overlap that helps drive a major question for American Muslims and the greater Muslim ummah (community): how far can American Islam go in its inevitable break with traditional Islam? At one extreme, there is the post-9/11 presence of Muslim punk-rock music, performed by American groups like the Kominas, who consider themselves good musicians and good Muslims. They know that their music – complete with Mohawks, leather jackets, loud guitars, heavy drumbeats, biting lyrics, and lots and lots of shouting – offends conservative Muslims ('Satanic music,' said one critic[6]) but the musicians do it anyway, and their concerts draw scores of other Muslims, including hijab-wearing women who dance raucously next to men. Is this *haram* (prohibited by Islam)? No, the musicians say, arguing that the Quran and the Sunnah don't prohibit music. The Kominas, whose name means 'scum-bag' in Punjabi, were started by South Asian-American Muslims in their twenties, including Shahjehan Khan, who grew up in the Boston area. The group's hits include such songs as 'Sharia Law in the USA' and 'Suicide Bomb the GAP'. In its quest to prove the band's bona fides, the Kominas debated with a devout Muslim man in front of a Massachusetts mosque in 2007, filming the episode and putting it on YouTube,[7] where it has been seen by thousands of people. 'You're telling me what I'm doing is un-Islamic, when that's for me to decide – it's between me and God,' Khan tells the mosque-goer. 'There are numerous examples in the Quran and the Sunnah of parties, of dancing, of celebration, of music.' After leaving the mosque, Khan – on the subject of convincing other Muslims about music – says to the camera: 'We have to wage intellectual jihad.'

This intellectual pursuit – instigated by musicians, writers, artists, scholars, and other activists – is taking place across the United States, but for every Shahjehan Khan there is a Zachary Adam Chesser: a Muslim-American who pushes the limits on how far other Americans – Muslim or non-Muslim – can go in presenting a dissenting view of Islam. In April 2010, Chesser issued a warning that the creators of the popular *South Park* comedy TV show might be murdered for the way they represented the Prophet Muhammad. The animated show had satirized the debate over whether Muhammad could be depicted in the kind of controversial cartoons that were published in the Danish newspaper *Jyllands-Posten*. One *Jyllands-Posten* cartoon showed Muhammad with a bomb in his turban. *South Park* showed Muhammad as a stick figure in a drawing, and as a person completely enveloped in the suit of a bear with big eyes, smiling face, and tongue sticking out. A convert to Islam,

Chesser – going by his Arabic name, Abu Talhah al-Amrikee – said the *South Park* creators, Trey Parker and Matt Stone, 'will probably wind up like Theo Van Gogh for airing this show'[8] – a reference to the Dutch filmmaker who was knifed to death for making a film that showed semi-naked women with Quranic verses on their skin. Two months after his warning, Chesser – a follower of the radical American cleric Anwar al-Awlaki – was arrested by US authorities, and pled guilty to multiple charges, including encouraging people to kill Parker and Stone.

Chesser's threats, and the *South Park* episode, sparked a national discussion among American Muslims about the place of Islam in the United States. Most Muslim groups condemned the threats to the creators of *South Park*, but the show still made Muslim-Americans uneasy, and forced then to explain that Islam prohibits images of Muhammad (and other prophets), although some historical Islamic texts have shown Muhammad's face. For many Americans, this prohibition on imagery is hard to comprehend given how often Jewish and Christian prophets are depicted in popular culture. The *South Park* controversy, and the subsequent one over 'Everybody Draw Muhammad Day' – a day that its US organizers hoped would attract millions of supporters for free speech – emphasized the religious and cultural breach that exists between American Muslims and their non-Muslim compatriots.

American Muslims like Virginia Gray Henry, a publisher and author in Kentucky, say they have an obligation to bridge that divide. Henry's personal timeline connects such disparate figures as George Washington, 1960s American guru Timothy Leary, and the Dalai Lama with American Islam. With Leary, the Harvard lecturer who took psychedelic drugs and urged people to 'Turn on, tune in, drop out', and such other 1960s notables as the Grateful Dead, Henry worked on a movie that she calls a 'big psychedelic film'. But Henry, who, as an undergraduate at New York's Sarah Lawrence College, did stage work for singer Janis Joplin's performances, says of the 1960s: 'What had started out as a beautiful movement of Flower Power became just a bunch of kids taking drugs.' Searching for a new spiritual direction, Henry found it in Islam. As director of the interfaith publishing house Fons Vitae in Louisville, Kentucky, she publishes books such as *What Is Sufism?*, *Islam in Tibet*, and *Understanding Islam and the Muslims*. In 2006, she organized a conference in San Francisco between the Dalai Lama and American Muslims. The Dalai Lama told the gathering, 'Nowadays to some people the Muslim tradition appears more militant. I feel that's totally wrong. Muslims, like any other traditions – same message, same practice. That is a practice of compassion.'[9]

Though Henry's familial connection to Patrick Henry is the most notable one in her family, she told me another side of her family has a connection to Washington and to the president's famous military move that surprised the British and turned the war in the American colonies' favor. 'My Gray side came to Virginia in the 1600s,' she said. 'During the Revolutionary War, a descendant, George Gray, put all his money into outfitting men, and joined the crossing of the Delaware. George Washington gave him 5,000 acres of distant land in Virginia.' That land became part of Kentucky, and it's where Gray grew up and still lives in Louisville, where, she says with a matter-of-factness, 'We have six mosques.'

American Islam is in a transition period. Though Muslims have lived in America for at least 400 years, it has only been in the last 40 years – after the loosening of immigration laws in 1965, highlighted by the Hart–Celler Act – that Muslims became a population that did not look back. The majority of American Muslims (65 percent) are first-generation immigrants,[10] according to the 2007 survey by the Pew Research Center. Around half of all US mosques date from the 1980s and 1990s,[11] according to the 2001 survey orchestrated by the Council on American-Islamic Relations. Compared to Muslims in the Middle East, American Muslims are less religious. According to the Gallup Center for Muslim Studies, 80 percent of American Muslims say religion plays an important part in their lives, compared to 100 percent for Muslims in Egypt, 96 percent in Saudi Arabia, 96 percent in Jordan, and 86 percent in Lebanon.[12]

Almost half (47 percent) of US Muslims think of themselves as Muslim first, not American,[13] according to a 2007 survey by the Pew Research Center. Compared to Europe, though, the numbers are low: In Britain, more than three-quarters of Muslims (81 percent) consider themselves Muslim first, not British; in Spain, it's 69 percent, in Germany it's 66 percent, and in France it's 46 percent.[14]

American Islam, of course, doesn't exist in isolation. What happens in America often has an effect around the world – for better or for worse. When Terry Jones, a fringe pastor in Florida, threatened to burn Qurans on the 2010 anniversary of the 9/11 attacks because: 'This book is responsible for 9/11',[15] protests around the world ensued. The 'Ground Zero mosque' controversy, which reached a crescendo around the same time as Jones' threatened burning, also generated heated international discussion. At a discussion on American Islam days before the anniversary, Akbar S. Ahmed, a Pakistani-born professor at American University in Washington, DC, spoke with *Washington Post* journalist Sally Quinn, who remarked that, 'The whole issue about what's happening with Islam in America has really been brought to a head by these two events [the proposed New York Islamic center and the threatened Quran burning].

And this is what everyone is talking about. Islam in America is a huge issue, and something that resonates all over the world. It's not just in this country.'[16]

As it resonates around the world, American Islam also confuses since there are paradoxical realities. Generally speaking, Americans distrust Muslims more than any other major religious group. In its 2009 report, 'Religious Perceptions in America: With an In-Depth Analysis of U.S. Attitudes Toward Muslims and Islam', the Gallup world survey found that 43 percent of Americans felt at least 'a little' prejudice against Muslims[17] (compared to 18 percent expressing at least a little hatred against Christians, and 15 percent expressing prejudice against Jews and Buddhists).[18] However, the United States is one of the top countries in the world for conversions to Islam. Around 30,000 people a year convert to the religion, according to *The American Mosque 2011* poll.[19]

This bi-polar existence is a fact of life for Muslim-Americans, who have to navigate it every day. Some Muslims avoid the public slaloming they would otherwise have to do by anglicizing their Muslim names – from Fareed to Fred, for example – or by never admitting their faith in public. I interviewed a prominent white American who had converted to Islam many years ago, but who told me to keep the religious switch off the record. Why? Because this person believed the people in her area would look askance at her, and her social connections would suffer as a result. More than a third of Muslim-Americans (37 percent) say they are 'very' or 'somewhat' worried about being rejected for a job position because of their faith.[20]

Still, Americans who convert to Islam often take the opposite approach – they're so exuberant about their new religion that they're happy to inform others they are Muslim. When I visited the Islamic Center of Moscow in the state of Idaho, Adam Frey

– a former Christian who has been a Muslim since 2004 – told me it was important for his new faith to be represented in a state with a long history of white supremacist groups, though he quickly added that Muslims had been welcomed by people in Moscow, Idaho. Because the University of Idaho has its campus in Moscow, the city has a more diverse population than other parts of Idaho. When I met with Frey at the Islamic center, he brought his friend from the mosque, Sherif El-Badawy, a civil engineer and post-doctoral fellow at the university who was born and raised in Egypt. El-Badawy, who did graduate work at the Arizona State University, told me that Islam in America has come a long way in a short time. 'In the Phoenix area,' he says, 'there are maybe seven or eight mosques pretty close to each other, within 20 square miles. I think there were about 8,000 Muslims there. From my apartment, I could choose from any of the eight. All of them were within 20 minutes' drive.'

Frey, who is 45, says his connection to Islam began when he went to the Central Asian country of Kyrgyzstan in 2003, to meet a Chechnyan woman he had met on the internet. He didn't know she was Muslim; he didn't know his attraction to her would ultimately bring him to Islam. 'She was my first direct exposure to Muslims,' Frey says.

She had been a Communist, but her family had a more religious bent to them. It sparked something in my mind. These people are so kind – they're relatively poor, especially by our standards – but they'd give you the shirt off their back. They're gracious hosts. You just couldn't ask for nicer people. I thought, 'What is it that they know? What is it that I'm missing?' That got me on a spiritual quest. I was reaching an age – I was pushing 40 – where I was asking, 'Where am I going? What am I doing?' The questions we all ask ourselves, hopefully, at some point.

Soon after his birth, Frey had been adopted by a couple through the Catholic Church in Denver, Colorado, but 'even though I was raised Catholic, I never bought into the Trinity,' he says.

> I always prayed to God and God alone – that there was no God but God. I knew that murder was wrong, and fornication was wrong, and charity was good. So Islam was not so much of a radical switch for me. It was simply doing more of what I knew deep down inside. I just didn't have the instructional manual.

The 'manual' for Islam – the Quran, the Sunnah, and other religious texts and traditions – has guided Frey not just in religion but in familial matters. He married the Chechnyan woman, but – in a development he calls 'really ironic' – he adopted a more conservative approach to Islam, and 'she wasn't as conservative or committed as I wanted her to be.' Their relationship broke up, and – 'alhamdulilah,' Frey says, using the Arabic phrase for 'God be praised' – he met a more religious woman, from Egypt, who wears the niqab, or full veil. They were married in 2006.

Love frequently leads people to convert to another faith – whether it is Islam, Judaism, Christianity, or other religion – but the high number of American conversions to Islam can be traced to the country's openness to different faiths, to its complicated beginnings (when slavery was an institution), and to Islam's own racial openness, says Zaid Shakir, a prominent African-American scholar who converted to Islam in 1977. Historically, the United States is a country that allows 'second chances' – it allows people the opportunity to reinvent any aspect of their identity, including religion.

'Number one,' Shakir tell me,

you don't have an entrenched sense of tradition that you have, say, in Western Europe. Then you have a society that's made up of immigrants. Then you have, at the very least, three very diverse traditions or narratives: the tradition of the European immigrant who was fleeing persecution or whatever they were fleeing in Europe; the tradition of the African slave; and the native people whose story is integral to this country. These are three very unique people racially, with three very different foundational narratives, coming together in one place, and all of them are integral to the formation of the country. And the country is only 200 years old, so you don't have the entrenched centuries of inherited tradition. With the very diverse foundational narratives, a person doesn't feel like he or she is an apostate to an entrenched sense of tradition when they become Muslim in America. Or a person doesn't feel – because the country itself is so diverse racially and ethnically – that if you become a Muslim you're a traitor to your race, if you will. Those are very real things. In Europe, for example, a convert would have to negotiate all of that psychologically, emotionally, to really get to a position – and people do – to work through all of that, whereas here you don't really have to work through that.

America's tradition of resistance movements – led by whites and blacks – also dovetails with Islam's, so Americans looking to break free from their past find a parallel in the religion, Shakir says. These traditions stretch back as far as the country itself. 'You have Daniel Shays [in 1786] resisting the corruption of the bankers and the big landowners in Boston,' says Shakir.

You have the history of the Wobblies and Socialists and Communist movements in this country. That's in the white community where you have dissidents. Then you have a history of very strong resistance among African-Americans. And then

Native Americans – their whole narrative is a narrative of resistance, even though the story didn't turn out too well for them. Still, the narrative is one of resistance. There are a lot of people in the country. And when they become disenchanted they began looking for ways to express that disenchantment, and for a lot of people, Islam becomes a means of expressing some disenchantment. Maybe you're disenchanted with the racial situation, and you study Islam. At least in theory, and to a certain extent in practice, you find a far more appealing philosophy and practice of race relations. So that attracts you. Or maybe spiritually you're disenchanted, and you feel that just the crass materialism that we find here – the consumerism is weighing you down – and you start studying Islam, and especially if you're studying more on the Sufi side it's a very refined spiritual system, so that attracts you. So there are a lot of aspects and elements of Islam that attract people who might be disenchanted with various elements of the dominant society, and the dominant social structure, and the dominant ethos.

However, even converts who embrace Islam bring with it their own traditions, and this is why Islam in America – at least the practice of the religion and the embodiment of its faith – is different from the way it is practiced elsewhere, in small and big ways. A small way, for example, is that Islam prohibits the marking of the body for ornamentation, but in the United States many convert Muslims have tattoos. Frey has them on his arms. So does America's most notable Muslim calligrapher, Mohamed Zakariya, who designed the 'Eid Greetings' postage stamp released by the US government in the weeks before 9/11. Like Frey, Zakariya got his tattoos before converting to Islam. And like Frey, he's not having them removed. Zakariya's stem from his years as a professional tattooist in the early 1960s. 'Mine are kinds of hodgepodges – mostly bunches of flowers and stuff like that,' he once told me.[21] 'I have a small dragon somewhere, and a snake, but most of them are just flowers.' Asked why he hasn't removed them in the 40 years since converting to Islam, Zakariya laughed and said: 'You couldn't do it well; it meant enormous scarring. On the other hand, I never cried about spilt milk. There's no point in trying to erase them.'

US-born Muslims – converts and those brought up in the faith – don't want to erase their identities as 'Americans', in whatever personal way that means to them. For Muslims in America, this has led to competing visions of their faith – a situation that really became noticeable after the 1960s and 1970s immigration influx, which brought Muslims from around the world to the United States. The influx also brought funding of mosques and organizations from Qatar, Egypt, Saudi Arabia, and other Muslim-majority countries. Imams came from abroad, too, so that American Islam in this period – until the 1990s – had a strong emphasis on foreign-born leaders who tended to be conservative in outlook. The Muslim Students Association, the Islamic Society of North America and other prominent US organizations were founded in this period. African-American Muslims were on another track until 1975, when Warith Deen Muhammad revamped the Nation of Islam into a Sunni-oriented organization – but even then, African-American Muslims were often estranged from their fellow American Muslims, praying in different mosques, and emphasizing different social agendas. It has been the next generation of American Muslims – men and women in their thirties, forties, and fifties who studied Islam in more prestigious institutions or otherwise reached higher levels of Islamic understanding – that have tried to transform the way Islam is practiced in America. Many of these Muslims were born or raised in the United States, and they're reconciling the traditions of their religion with the realities of American life. Zaytuna College, which opened in 2010, is a prime example of this more 'indigenous Islam'. Started by Hamza Yusuf and Shakir – two prominent American-born converts who spent years at prestigious schools in the Middle East and North Africa – the school is training students in Islamic law and theology. For four years, undergraduates are required to learn Arabic, Islamic history, Quranic sciences, hadith sciences, economics, English composition, rhetoric, American history, Islamic business law, and other subjects, giving the students a grounding in American liberal arts and Islamic studies. Zaytuna's first class of 15 students included several who turned down Ivy League colleges to attend the Berkeley school. Male and female students freely speak to each other, and sit next to each other, without reticence, and the school emphasizes what it calls 'a free exchange of ideas'. Eventually, Zaytuna wants to produce imams and scholars who will filter Islam through the same liberal, theologically sound foundation. Zaytuna has received nearly all of its funding from American sources, the college says.

'In terms of the Muslim Students Association and other organizations, a lot of money – not the majority – but a significant amount of money in the past has come from overseas,' Shakir tells me.

> In the post-9/11 world, where there's a lot more hesitancy on the part of various donors to spend their money in America and to donate to Muslim causes here, there is an increasingly urgent sense that we definitely have to go it alone financially.

For Qazwini, who is also seeking to train the next generation of American imams, financing can be more flexible since the college that he and his family runs is in Karbala, Iraq. The seminary, which had an enrollment of students from the United States, Canada, and Europe, was supposed to open in 2009, but Iraq's tenuous security put the school on hold for at least two years. 'This seminary caters to Western Muslims, so they can return and preach Islam – moderate Islam – in the West,' Qazwini tells me.

We decided to wait until things settle down. Otherwise, the building is ready. It's complete. It cost over half a million dollars to finish the building in Karbala. We have the plan to accept 30 students every year. Even the expenses will be covered by the seminary itself. These students go and do not worry about anything other than studying.

Qazwini says it does not matter how people label the type of Islam that's practiced by Muslims in America. What is more important, he says, is that the religion embraces the diversity that is inherent in the United States. 'Some people may call it "liberal Islam",' Qazwini tells me.

Some people call it 'moderate Islam'. Some people call it 'diverse Islam'. We live in a diverse society where Muslims don't live by themselves. There are Christians, Jews, Hindus, you name it. With the co-existence of these denominations, the idea came to be more tolerable toward our differences as Americans. And therefore, we as Muslims, we believe these practices – separation but not segregation, for example – may help integrate Muslims into the bigger society. And that, in the end, we are Muslim, but we would like to be integrated in the society. We don't want to be assimilated *or* isolated. And I believe part of integration is to adopt the practice that can preserve our identity as Muslims yet it does not keep us too far from the society that we live in. And I believe that these practices that Muslims are having are very key to the idea of diversity in the United States.

Ideally, this diversity would bring together American Muslims and non-Muslims in unprecedented ways – which it has. Among Americans of South Asian descent, for example, intermarriages between Muslims and Hindus have happened – a commingling that rarely happens in South Asia itself. Muslims and Jews have married on American soil. Scores of American interfaith organizations have sprouted up in the past 20 years, including the Interfaith Dialog Center, started in New Jersey by Turkish-Americans; the Interfaith and Community Alliance, begun by America's largest Muslim group, the Islamic Society of North America; and the Arizona Interfaith Movement, on whose board sits M. Zuhdi Jasser, a Muslim doctor of Syrian descent who was a lieutenant commander in the United States Navy. The American Islamic Congress, started by moderate Muslims in the wake of 9/11, has published a guideline for Muslims who want to get involved in interfaith work, and the guideline reminds its readers that 'Interfaith dialogue – in its American context – is in many ways a new phenomenon for Islam.'[22]

The phenomenon happened because Islam is a minority religion in America, and because Muslims themselves realized they needed to do a better job of interacting with other religions, and within their religion. Interfaith dialogue has often meant Shia and Sunni Muslims meeting to discuss their differences, and Muslims of South Asian descent meeting with African-American Muslims. What has happened in America more than any other country is that the level of public frankness has increased. In 2008, Azhar Usman – a Chicago comedian born to Muslim immigrants from India – published 'An Apology' that was the talk of American Muslims. The essay – more serious than funny – was written after the death of Warith Deen Muhammad, who guided African-American Muslims for 30 years. Usman's mea culpa apologized for the way that South Asian, Arab, and other 'immigrant Muslims' in the United States had, for decades, treated African-American Muslims.[23] Usman's essay apologized for the 'self-righteous way' that immigrant Muslims questioned the religious adherence of African-American Muslims – how immigrant Muslims would tell African-American Muslims that 'your beard is not quite Sunnah enough, or your outfit is not quite Islamic enough, or your Koranic recitation is not quite Arabic enough.'[24]

The divisiveness that Usman described persists because these different Muslim communities have such different histories in the United States, and because of initial distrust that has lingered in these communities. In *New Faiths, Old Fears: Muslims and Other Asian Immigrants in American Religious Life*, Bruce Lawrence, director of Duke University's Islamic Studies Center, notes what he calls the

persistence of cultural disparities, despite creedal and ritual sympathies, between indigenous African American and immigrant, largely South Asian, Muslim communities. The major impediment to collective solidarity among Muslims remains internalized racial prejudice [...] Racialized class prejudice runs deep, even in the face of a universal religious ethos that eschews race as a marker of worth, even among American Muslims in the twenty-first century.[25]

Usman's essay tried to subvert this raw history in one setting. One section read:

For every Pakistani doctor who can find money in his budget to drive a Lexus and live in a million-dollar house in suburbia, and who has the audacity to give Friday sermons about the virtues of Brotherhood in Islam, while the Black mosque can't pay the heating bills or provide enough money to feed starving Muslim families just twenty miles away, I'm sorry.

And for every Arab speaker in America who makes it his business to raise millions and millions of dollars to provide 'relief' for Muslim refugees around the world, but turns a blind eye to the plight of our very own Muslim sisters and brothers right here in our American inner cities just because, in his mind, the color black might as well be considered invisible, I'm sorry.[26]

Among American Muslims, Usman's essay was met with applause, a few critical remarks, and – because he had used levity – some laughs. Among non-Muslims, Usman is a pioneer: through his stand-up act and many TV appearances, he's usually the first funny Muslim who has made them laugh. (One Usman joke is about the Muslim greeting 'Salaam aleykum'. In it, Usman acts like a non-Muslim who misunderstands what he hears: 'Salami and bacon? I thought you don't eat pork.')

Born and raised in Illinois, Usman was inspired to be a comic by America's culture of comedy – from the open-mic nights at night clubs to the TV shows like *Saturday Night Live* that showcase topical humor about news and popular culture. A former writer for *Saturday Night Live*, Preacher Moss, was – with Usman – the creator of the 'Allah Made me Funny' tour that took a trio of stand-up Muslim comics around the United States and then, when it became successful, to different parts of the world, including Europe and the Middle East. A theatrical movie of the tour and a DVD version further enhanced Usman's (and Moss') reputation for doing 'Muslim comedy' at a high professional level. In many ways, Usman's performances are a kind of *da`wa* – an invitation to get to know a side of the

Muslim world that non-Muslims (and even fellow Muslims) may be unfamiliar with. The tradition of humor is an important one in Islam, dating to the time of the Prophet Muhammad, who had people who were essentially court jesters, Hamza Yusuf, who is friends with Usman, once told me.[27] American Islam is thus reviving – for the twenty-first century – a tradition that had been winnowed out over the centuries.

This tradition could be heard in the voice of Mehdi Khorasani, a Persian cleric from Karbala, Iraq, who for decades led the Islamic Society of California in Marin County, a wealthy enclave across the Golden Gate Bridge from San Francisco. One of the funniest (and most philosophical) Muslims who achieved prominence in the United States, Khorasani – who was from a prominent Shiite family in Iraq – used aphorisms, analogies, and humor to explain Islam to visitors. Wearing the black turban that indicated his lineage connects to the Prophet Muhammad, Khorasani told me when I once visited him that he regularly invited non-Muslims inside the mosque to give them advice or to let them see the inside of a Muslim house of worship. 'I opened it for everyone – Buddhists, Hindus, Jews, anyone,' he told me.[28] 'When I feed this little cat,' he said, pointing to a feline walking by his leg, 'I don't ask, "Are you a Muslim?" I feed him, and I let him drink, and he enjoys.' In 2010 when I spoke with him again, I asked if he was considering going back to Iraq. Then in his seventies, Khorasani told me, laughing a little: 'My heart is there; my body won't go there.'

Many Muslims who arrived in America in the mid to late twentieth century did not plan on staying. They were fleeing strife in their homelands and seeking economic opportunities, and they wanted to eventually return to their countries of birth. Not anymore. Islam has planted its roots firmly in the United States. In New York, Washington, DC, and other major cities

of America, the presence of mosques old and new spotlight this
turnaround, and are the clearest signs of Islam's ascendance in
the land of Thomas Jefferson and Abraham Lincoln. In many
ways, though, it is the out-of-the-way mosques – in places like
Fairfax, California and Moscow, Idaho – that are more profound
exemplars of Islam in America. Khorasani's mosque is nicknamed
the Redwood Mosque because it sits in a redwood grove of trees
that date back hundreds and hundreds of years, to a time when
Spaniards and Native Americans were the only people who lived
in the area. Khorasani bought the property in 1974.

The Islamic Center of Moscow is the first mosque in the city of
20,000 that is best known for its historic downtown, arts events
(including the Lionel Hampton International Jazz Festival), old
churches, surrounding farmlands, and the University of Idaho
(founded in 1889). Only 50 or so people regularly pray at the
Islamic Center of Moscow, and on the day that I visited, just
Frey and El-Badawy were there for the *dhuhr* prayer (the one
just after noon). The center's prayer space is slightly bigger than
a room in a studio apartment. On one wall was a calendar from
the Muslim ummah of North America, a self-described social
and da`wa organization; a blackboard that advertised a local
farm with lambs for sale; and a certificate from the state of
Idaho acknowledging 'the Muslim Community of the Palouse'
(Palouse is an area that overlaps Moscow) for its volunteer
cleaning of roadways from 2003 to 2009. On another wall was a
photo of the Kaaba, the holy black stone in Mecca that Muslims
are obligated to pray toward. That was what Frey and El-Badawy
were doing, facing Mecca as they went through the prayer rituals
that millions of Muslims do five times a day. On this day, Frey
was the de facto prayer leader, leading El-Badawy in words
('Subhaana ala humma wa bihamdika') and motion as they bent
up and down in unison.

Later, I spoke with them near Moscow's Main Street, in a café where patchouli oil enveloped the air, the music of Billie Holiday played in the background, and a student crowd occupied the tables around us. Some of the women there were wearing revealing clothing. 'My wife', says Frey, 'wouldn't be caught dead in here.' Frey puts up with the café scene. He wears a long beard in the tradition of conservative Islam, though he retains some of his old habits, including riding a Harley-Davidson motorcycle and dressing in jeans and long-sleeved shirts that are checked and flannel. 'I don't look like a Muslim,' Frey says.

> I have a beard, but this is Idaho. I could be a lumberjack. I'm heavily tattooed, so people don't assume I'm a Muslim. A lot of times I'm in a conversation [with non-Muslims], and one of them will make a sexist remark or a racist remark. They'll use the N-word. And they'll say, 'We elected a blank for a president [referring to Barack Obama].' And they expect me to agree because of my appearance. They'll call me 'white brother'. Then I tell them I'm a Muslim.

That is where the conversation turns. Many of the people Frey meets have never met a Muslim before, and they are often embarrassed that their prejudices have been revealed. Frey is not embarrassed for them. He likes engaging them in discussions about religion and culture, and challenging their beliefs. Sometimes, they will tell Frey that Islam is 'sick' since it allows men to have more than one wife. 'Secular people who think it's cool to have two girlfriends or to sleep around with a different woman every night – well, God forbid if you have two wives who you live with in a state of matrimony and you support,' Frey says.

Throughout history, polygamy has often been a means – because of war, when there's a shortage of men – a legitimate answer. It still is. Go to Chechnya. Go to Iraq. There are so many women who can't take care of children because their husband has been killed. What's the problem with men taking care of two wives?

Frey says his wife, whose niqab covers her entire face except for eye space, is always stared at in the town. 'People think she's oppressed, but she has the US equivalent of a master's degree,' he says.

She is a professional. She comes from a noble family. People think she's strange for covering her face, but a woman can walk around town half-naked and that's OK – but to be modest and to cover yourself so you don't cause a distraction to men, and you believe to preserve your beauty for your husband, this is considered abnormal?

Frey lets the question hang in the air. The debate about Islam and Islam's presence on the American continent has existed for more than 300 years. Like other Muslims, Frey thinks the United States is an ideal country for Islam. He says,

In some ways, America is more Islamic than Muslim countries. I mean the spirit of things. I've traveled all over the Middle East. Yemen. Saudi Arabia. Turkey. Morocco. Jordan. And, in America, the sense of fairness, justice, openness, honesty – these are Islamic values. I don't have to pay bribes here. If I'm pulled over by a police officer, chances are it's legitimate – I did something wrong. Maybe I can explain things; maybe he'll let me off. But I don't offer him $20 and he lets me go. That's exactly what happens in much of the Muslim world. And this is a very un-Islamic practice, going on in the midst of Muslims. It's from the *lack* of religion there.

Qazwini might agree with Frey. Like Frey, Qazwini has experienced the religion in many countries beyond the United States, including Saudi Arabia. He tells me that the Prophet Muhammad foresaw the religion reaching all corners of the world. The American continent was not known in Muhammad's time, but the United States has more Muslims than lived in the Arabian Peninsula during Muhammad's time in the sixth and seventh centuries.

'Muhammad envisioned in many of his sayings that Islam will be disseminated around the world,' Qazwini tells me. 'And in some sayings that are reported by Muslims from the Prophet Muhammad, the Prophet indicates that the words of Islam will reach the furthest point on earth in the future. He did not say when. He just referred to the future.'

The future is now. The religion that was revealed to Muhammad is the same religion that Qazwini and Frey carry with them in Dearborn, Michigan and Moscow, Idaho and wherever they go in the United States. Qazwini, an imam in America's most Arabic city who is a descendant of the Prophet Muhammad, and Frey, a white convert living in America's remote northwest whose family lineage is unclear, say they have the same goal: to be ambassadors for their faith in a country that originally only welcomed Muslims if they were slaves. America's first Muslims were perceived as less than human – people put in chains, forced to do field work at gunpoint, required to take new names and a new religion. So much has changed in 400 years, even if the struggle for acceptance is an ongoing one. Muslim-Americans say they even envision a day when the president of the United States is a Muslim. In American politics, there had not been an elected Muslim member of Congress – an august body that dates back to 1774 – until Keith Ellison was voted to office in 2007. In 2008, a second Muslim, Andre Carson, was elected to Congress, from the state of Indiana, and Carson and Ellison have since been re-elected. Historically, in the most visible areas of peacetime American life (politics, pop culture, sports, and media), Muslim figures were few or non-existent in the upper echelons. So in terms of popular 'mainstream' culture, Americans have generally not encountered positive representations of Islam. What Americans have encountered is widespread media coverage of turbulence in the Muslim world, and of America's conflicts in Muslim lands. Whether it was the 1979 Iranian revolution, which led to a prolonged standoff involving US hostages, or the post-9/11 wars in Iraq and Afghanistan, which led to tens of thousands of soldier and civilian deaths, a kind of 'war-torn Islam' was brought into America's living rooms, which colored the perception of the religion and of American Muslims themselves. Was Islam even compatible with idealized American values of democracy? Did Muslims even belong in a country that, according to many Americans, is 'Judeo-Christian' in origin?

These are the questions that American Muslims have to face over and over – if not to their faces then in the subtext of public discussions about their religion. For better or worse, the terrorist attacks of 9/11 put American Islam in a vast spotlight, and put American Muslims on the defensive, prompting them to examine not just their own lives but the lives of Muslim-Americans who came before them – people who were their religious antecedents and who 'proved' that Islam had a long, peacetime trajectory on American soil. The history of American Islam stretches back to before George Washington, Thomas Jefferson, and other founding fathers declared the United States a sovereign country independent of Great Britain.

When Yvonne Yazbeck Haddad, professor of history of Islam and Christian–Muslim relations at Georgetown University's Center for Muslim–Christian Understanding, used the word 'indigenous' to describe American Muslims – as she did in the 1991 book, *The Muslims of America*, when she wrote that Muslims were becoming 'increasingly an indigenous part of America'[29] – she emphasized a crucial point: American Islam has never been static, and this untethered state provides the impetus for American Islam to continue evolving in a unique way. In *The Muslims of America*, Haddad wrote that US Muslims who emigrated from Muslim-majority countries were particularly vulnerable to culture shock:

> The American experience has presented Muslims with a special challenge. They have unprecedented freedom to experiment with forms and structures for the separation of religion and state away from the watchful eyes of wary governments and the criticism of traditionalists. At the same time, this freedom is fraught with the danger of innovation and deviance; the great range of options available in the American context carries the threat of sectarian division and fragmentation.[30]

Twenty years after Haddad typed those words, sectarian division and fragmentation have been kept to a relative minimum. American Islam has segmented the same way that Islam has segmented in other countries – Sunni vs. Shia, Salafi vs. Sufi – but that segmentation has never seriously erupted into intra-Muslim violence. The United States' tradition of public forums and open debate has encouraged discussion of issues that, in Muslim-majority countries, would be more volatile and threatening. One example is the issue of the hijab, and whether practicing Muslim women are obligated to wear the head covering that indicates piousness. This has become more noted in the American mainstream as more hijab-wearing women such as Dalia Mogahed, one-time advisor to President Barack Obama, obtain positions of public prominence, and as more US Muslim women who eschew the hijab become better known.

Rima Fakih, the Lebanese-born winner of the 2010 Miss USA beauty pageant, not only goes without a hijab but frequently makes public appearances wearing outfits that show off bare shoulders. Fakih's Twitter account – which has more than 175,000 followers – features a photo of her in a provocative pose, and Fakih sends out such tweets as 'Ramadan Mubarak' ('Blessed Ramadan').[31] Fakih, who says she fasts during Ramadan, spent her teenage years in Dearborn, Michigan, a Detroit suburb where a third of the population (about 33,000 people) claim Arab ancestry, giving Dearborn the distinction of having the highest percentage of Arab-Americans in the United States. *All-American Muslim*, the first reality TV series about Muslim-American families, which aired on the American cable television channel TLC in 2011 and 2012, was centered in Dearborn. The series featured men, women, and children who were navigating the intersection between religious principles and secular pursuits, as in the family of Mohsen and Lila Amen, long-time Dearborn residents who have one daughter, Shadia, who disregards the hijab, has visible tattoos, and is engaged to an Irish-Catholic man who is converting to Islam to marry her. Mohsen and Lila's two other daughters are devout wearers of the hijab, as is Lila.

One of the five *All-American Muslim* families is headed by Fouad Zaban, the head football coach at Dearborn's Fordson High School, who when I spoke to him a few years earlier told me how his Muslim players incorporate Islamic chanting into their pre-game rituals. The chanting, Zaban says, includes Arabic pronouncements about Hussein ibn Ali, the seventh-century imam and grandson of the Prophet Muhammad, whose murder is remembered by Shia Muslims around the world on the tenth day of the Muslim month of Muharram. 'You know how they commemorate the martyrdom of Hussein, and they have those rituals and chants? That's pretty much what some of [my players] listen to,' Zaban told me.[32] 'At times during a game, when they feel it's time to do something really important – a big play, for example – they may say, 'God is the greatest', 'Allahu Akbar'. They do that before the actual play – something to motivate them.'

For the hundreds of thousands of people who watched *All-American Muslim*, the series became a window into Muslim America – a chance to debate how much these families are a microcosm of Islam in America, and how much beloved institutions like American football have been adopted by America's Muslim communities. The series erupted in controversy when a conservative Christian group, the Florida Family Association, which preaches what it calls 'traditional, biblical values', orchestrated a campaign to force companies to withdraw their advertising from the series, resulting in a major home-improvement chain, Lowe's, pulling out – and leading Keith Ellison and other Muslim-Americans to say the corporation gave in to dubious threats from a fringe organization. The Florida Family Association claimed *All-American Muslim* was

> propaganda designed to counter legitimate and present-day concerns about many Muslims who are advancing Islamic fundamentalism and Sharia law [in the United States]. The show profiled only Muslims that appeared to be ordinary folks while excluding many Islamic believers whose agenda poses a clear and present danger to liberties and traditional values that the majority of Americans cherish.[33]

The controversy re-exposed the historical fault line that is reinforced by Americans who hold disparaging views of Islam, but the controversy also showed how far Islam had come into the American mainstream. America's wittiest cable TV commentator, Jon Stewart of *The Daily Show*, teamed up with his show's 'Senior Muslim Correspondent', Aasif Mandvi, to lampoon Lowe's decision, with Mandvi calling – reluctantly, he joked – for Lowe's to be boycotted. Reluctantly because, Mandvi said, 'If there's one thing Muslims love more than terror, it's a bargain.'[34] The live TV audience at *The Daily Show* taping laughed uproariously at Mandvi's line. Humor is a cultural trait that American Muslims – at least comedic American Muslims – have specialized in, and it's a small but important example of how American Islam has evolved in unique ways. Stand-up comedy and riffing live with humor is an American tradition that second-generation Muslim-Americans – including Mandvi, Azhar Usman, and Dean Obeidallah, who is half-Palestinian and half-Italian – have embraced and, through touring, have brought to the Middle East, influencing Muslim comedy there. In 2011, Obeidallah was named one of the world's top 500 Muslims by Jordan's Royal Islamic Strategic Studies Centre,[35] which cited his work as executive director of the 2008 Amman Stand-Up Comedy Festival – the first stand-up comedy festival in the Middle East.

Who represents Islam in America? Scholars and religious authorities do not have a monopoly in the United States. The edges of Islam in America – edges that include Dean Obeidallah and Shadia Amen – are helping to define the religion as it is practiced in the United States. If America is still a melting pot of cultures, races, and religions, as it has been described for much of its history, then American Islam is also a melting pot that reflects the widest possible circle of what Islam has become. When slaves were brought to America 300 years ago, Ayuba Suleiman Ibrahima Diallo ('Job ben Solomon') and other Muslim captives were harassed and ridiculed if they prayed in public. Today, in addition to the mosques that dot American cities, Muslims will – as they do in Muslim-majority countries – pray outside if they find themselves there during any of the five required prayer times.

In the summer of 2011, I witnessed a man stop his car by a park in the Haight-Ashbury district of San Francisco, during a time when the dhuhr midday prayer was in effect, and saw him proceed to pray on the husks of cardboard boxes that had been left on the grass and dirt. Along the pathway that paralleled the man's impromptu prayer session in this central part of San Francisco, where the hippie movement was once centered, few pedestrians looked twice at his prostations toward Mecca. America's biggest outdoor prayer-gathering happens every year in New York City, during the city's Muslim Day Parade, which takes place on the last Sunday in September. Hundreds and hundreds of Muslim-Americans stroll along Madison Avenue – a famous boulevard that symbolizes America's advertising industry – and, during the dhuhr prayer, conduct a religious session in the street, where they kneel in unison and prostrate themselves toward the Kaaba. These New York Muslims touch their face to the ground, often atop a tarpaulin that becomes a giant prayer rug, as a muezzin chants, 'Allahu akbar . . . Allahu akbar.' Pedestrians who come across this collective gathering do stop and gawk, taking pictures with their camera phones. When the parade first began, in 1985, the outdoor prayers and the parade's moving floats (which feature such things as handicraft versions of the Kaaba) were anomalies. Even in 2007, Imam Shamsi Ali, co-chair of the parade, said that 'parades are a new thing in Islam.'[36] But non-Muslim New Yorkers have adjusted to the parade, and so have American Muslims. After one of the most recent parades, when the dhuhr prayer had ended, onlookers and prayer participants gathered their things and continued with their days. Many of the participants carried on with the parade. Many of the onlookers continued with their errands and Sunday routines. It was just another day when Islam was visible and people noticed but then went on with their lives. It was just another day in the United States of America.

Notes

Foreword
1 Lisa Miller, 'Islam in America: A Special Report', *Newsweek*, 20 July 2007. Available at www.newsweek.com/american-dreamers-islam-america-104633 (accessed 25 August 2014), quoted in Jane I. Smith, *Islam in America*, 2nd edn (New York, 2010), p. ix.
2 Karen Leonard, 'South Asian Leadership of American Muslims', in Yvonne Yazbeck Haddad (ed.), *Muslims in the West: From Sojourners to Citizens* (New York, 2002), pp. 235–6.
3 Robert Dannin, *Black Pilgrimage to Islam* (New York, 2002), p. 166.
4 Ibid., p. 175.
5 Ibid.
6 Ibid., p. 182.

Preface
1 Ihsan Bagby, *The American Mosque 2011: Report Number 1 from the US Mosque Study 2011* (n.p., 2012), p. 5.
2 The US census does not ask citizens about religion, so there are no official governmental statistics on the number of American Muslims. Estimates are based on polls by national organizations. At the high end in 1960, the Federation of Islamic Associations in America estimated the US Muslim population at 1.2 million. (See Ilyas Ba-Yunus, *Muslims in America* (Westport, CT, 2006), p. 28). In 2007, the Pew Research Center estimated the population at 2.35 million. See Chapter 6 for a detailed discussion of the issue.
3 Andrea Elliott, 'In a Suspicious U.S., Muslim Converts Find Discrimination', *New York Times*, B1, 30 April 2005.

4 Bagby, *The American Mosque 2011*, p. 12.

5 John Esposito and Ibrahim Kalin (eds), *The 500 Most Influential Muslims*, (Amman, Jordan, 2009), p. 78.

6 Noam Cohen, 'With Brash Hosts, Headline News Finds More Viewers in Prime Time', *New York Times*, C1, 4 December 2006.

7 Timothy Marr, *The Cultural Roots of American Islamicism* (Cambridge, 2006), p. 21.

8 Worthington Chauncey Ford (ed.), *The Writings of George Washington, Vol. X, 1782–1785* (New York, 1891), p. 372.

9 Kevin J. Hayes, 'How Thomas Jefferson Read the Qur'ān,' *Early American Literature*, xxxix/2 (2004), p. 258.

10 Steven Waldman, *Founding Faith: Providence, Politics, and the Birth of Religious Freedom in America* (New York, 2008), p. 125. See also www.loc. gov/teachers/classroommaterials/connections/thomas-jefferson/history3. html (accessed 25 August 2014).

11 Frank Lambert, *The Founding Fathers and the Place of Religion in America* (Princeton, NJ, 2006), p. 239.

12 Alexis de Tocqueville, *Democracy in America*, trans. Henry Reeve (New York, 1900), p. 24.

13 Ralph Waldo Emerson, *The Later Lectures of Ralph Waldo Emerson, 1843–1871, Vol. II*, ed. Ronald A. Boso and Joel Myerson (Athens, GA, 2010), p. 285.

14 Rachel L. Swarns, 'Congressman Criticizes Election of Muslim,' *New York Times*, 31 December 2006, A31.

15 Thomas S. Kidd, *American Christians and Islam* (Princeton, NJ, 2009), p. 1.

1. Slavery and the Struggle to Maintain Belief

1 Allan D. Austin, *African Muslims in Antebellum America: A Sourcebook* (New York, 1984), p. 80. See also http://docsouth.unc.edu/neh/bluett/bluett.html (accessed 14 July 2014).

2 John L. Esposito, *What Everyone Needs to Know About Islam* (New York, 2011), p. 223.

3 Richard B. Marrin, *Runaways of Colonial New Jersey: Indentured Servants, Slaves, Deserters, and Prisoners, 1720–1781* (Westminster, MD, 2007), p. 22.

4 Ibid.

5 Robin Blackburn, *The Overthrow of Colonial Slavery, 1776–1848* (London, 1988), p. 128.

6 Thaddeus Mason Harris, *Biographical Memorials of James Oglethorpe: Founder of the Colony of Georgia in North America* (Boston, 1841), p. 30.

7 Ibid., p. 25.

8 Georgia Writers' Project, *Drums and Shadows: Survival Studies Among the Georgia Coastal Negroes* (Athens, GA, 1986), p. 166.

9 Bailey told me this in a 2004 interview for the *San Francisco Chronicle* that was included in the story, 'Muslim Roots of the Blues', published 15 August 2004, p. E1.

10 Michael A. Gomez, *Black Crescent: The Experience and Legacy of African Muslims in the Americas* (New York, 2005), p. 373.

11 Ibid.

12 Omar ibn Said, *Autobiography of Omar ibn Said, Slave in North Carolina, 1831,* ed. John Franklin Jameson, *American Historical Review,* xxx/4 (July 1925), pp. 787–95. Also available at http://docsouth.unc.edu/nc/omarsaid/omarsaid.html (accessed 14 July 2014). See also Jonathan Curiel, 'The Life of Omar ibn Said', *Saudi Aramco World,* March/April 2010, p. 34, and Ala Alryyes, *A Muslim American Slave: The Life of Omar Ibn Said* (Madison, WI, 2011), p. 18.

13 Said, *Autobiography of Omar ibn Said,* p. 794.

14 Curiel, 'The Life of Omar ibn Said'.

15 Said, *Autobiography of Omar ibn Said,* p. 793.

16 Terry Alford, *Prince Among Slaves: The True Story of an African Prince Sold into Slavery in the American South* (New York, 2007), p. 124.

17 Allan D. Austin, *African Muslims in Antebellum America: A Sourcebook* (New York, 1984), p. 142.

18 Jill Lepore, *A is for American: Letters and Other Characters in the Newly United States* (New York, 2002), p. 122.

19 Edward E. Curtis (ed.), *Encyclopedia of Muslim-American History* (New York, 2010), p. 543.

20 Mary-Jane Webb, 'Islam in America: Library Hosts Symposium on Muslim History, Culture in the U.S.', *Library of Congress Information Bulletin,* lvi/2 (February 2002). Available at www.loc.gov/loc/lcib/0202/islam-symp.html (accessed 14 July 2014).

21 Curtis, *Encyclopedia of Muslim-American History,* p. 317.

2. 'White Muslims' Change the Face of a Faith

1 'New-York's First Muezzin Call', *New York Times,* 11 December 1893, p. 1.

2 Paul Baepler, *White Slaves, African Masters: An Anthology of American Barbary Captivity Narratives* (Chicago, 1999), p. 69.

3 Ibid., p. 64.

4 Richard Zacks, *The Pirate Coast: Thomas Jefferson, the First Marines, and the Secret Mission of 1805* (New York, 2005), p. 275.

5 'Muhammed Webb's Mission: To Establish the Faith of Islam Here', *New York Times,* 25 February 1893, p. 1.

6 Umar F. Abd-Allah, *A Muslim in Victorian America: The Life of Alexander Russell Webb* (New York, 2006), p. 170.

7 Ibid.

8 Ibid., p. 174.

9 Kambiz GhaneaBassiri, *A History of Islam in America: From the New World to the New World Order* (New York, 2010), p. 163.

10 William Paul Dillingham, *Reports of the Immigration Commission: Dictionary of Races of Peoples* (Washington, DC, 1911), p. 30.

11 Ibid.

12 Ibid.

13 Ibid., p. 19.
14 'Muhammed Webb's Mission: To Establish the Faith of Islam Here,' *New York Times*.
15 Pew Research Center, *Muslim Americans: Middle Class and Mostly Mainstream* (Washington, DC, 2007), p. 24.
16 Philip Harsham, 'One Arab's Imagination', *Saudi Aramco World*, March/April 1975, p. 14.
17 John Henry Barrows (ed.), *The World's Parliament of Religions: An Illustrated and Popular Story of the World's First Parliament of Religions, Held in Chicago in Connection With the Columbian Exposition of 1893* (Chicago, 1893), p. 989.
18 Ibid.
19 Charles Carrol Everett (ed.), *The New World: A Quarterly Review of Religion, Ethics and Theology, Vol. III* (Boston and New York, 1894), p. 629.

3. Islam Becomes a Religion of the Nation

1 Madison Grant, *The Passing of the Great Race* (New York, 1936), p. xxix. Available at www.archive.org/stream/passingofgreatra00granuoft/passing ofgreatra00granuoft_djvu.txt (accessed 14 July 2014).
2 Ibid.
3 Ibid., p. xxxii.
4 Sarah F. Howell, 'Inventing the American Mosque: Early Muslims and their Institutions in Detroit, 1910–1980', PhD dissertation, University of Michigan, 2009, p. 158.
5 Ibid., p. 64.
6 David Greenberg, *Calvin Coolidge* (New York, 2006), p. 83.
7 John M. Murrin, *Liberty, Equality, Power: A History of the American People* (Boston, 2012), p. 667.
8 Grant, *The Passing of the Great Race*, p. xxviii.
9 'Building Islam in Detroit: Foundations/Forms/Futures, Panel 1', Building Islam in Detroit project, University of Michigan. Available at http://biid.lsa. umich.edu/exhibit-items/foundations-panel-1 (accessed 14 July 2014).
10 Edward E. Curtis (ed.), *The Columbia Sourcebook of Muslims in the United States* (New York, 2007), p. 59.
11 Robert Dannin, *Black Pilgrimage to Islam* (New York, 2002), p. 109.
12 Essien Udosen Essien-Udom, *Black Nationalism: A Search for an Identity in America* (Chicago, 1962), p. 71.
13 Ibid.
14 Adam Joel Banks, *Race, Rhetoric, and Technology: Searching for Higher Ground* (Mahwah, NJ, 2006), p. 54. See www.youtube.com/watch? v=7thXrDWhDDQ (accessed 14 July 2014).
15 Archie C. Epps (ed.), *The Speeches of Malcolm X at Harvard* (New York, 1968), p. 116.
16 Jane Otten, 'Islam Comes to Washington: Handsome New Mosque Unique Site for Tourists Visiting the Capital', *New York Times*, 8 August 1954, p. X21.

17 *Public Papers of the Presidents of the United States, Dwight D. Eisenhower, 1957,* General Services Administration, National Archives and Records Service, Federal Register Division, Washington, DC, 1958, p. 120.

18 'Vet Leads U.S. Moslems in Fight for Recognition; Founder of Society Meeting in Toledo Tells of Victorious Struggle with Army', *Toledo Blade,* 5 July 1953, p. 11.

19 Ilyas Ba-Yunus and Kassim Kone, *Muslims in the United States* (Westport, CT, 2006), p. 28.

20 Zahid Hussain Bukhari (ed.), *Muslims' Place in the American Public Square: Hope, Fears, and Aspirations* (Walnut Creek, CA, 2004), p. 300.

21 Herbert Aptheker, *Documentary History of the Negro People in the United States, Vol. VII: From the Alabama Protests to the Death of Dr. Martin Luther King, Jr.* (New York, 1994), p. 291.

22 Ibid.

23 Alan Stang, *It's Very Simple: The True Story of Civil Rights* (Boston, 1965), p. 65.

24 Edward J. Erler, Thomas G. West and John A. Marini, *The Founders on Citizenship and Immigration: Principles and Challenges in America* (Lanham, MD, 2007), p. 14.

4. Islam Establishes an Identity Far Beyond the Mosque

1 'ISNA's First President Ilyas Ba-Yunus Passed Away', *American Muslim Perspective* (online magazine), 5 October 2007. Available at http://archives 2007.ghazali.net/html/isna_president_passes_away.html (accessed 14 July 2014).

2 Mark Hamilton Purcell, *Recapturing Democracy* (New York, 2008), p. 51.

3 Lois Palken Rudnick, Judith E. Smith, and Rachel Rubin, *American Identities* (Malden, MA, 2006), p. 130.

4 'New Student Group Pickets White House', *New York Times,* 20 November 1961, p. 28.

5 Muslim Students Association of the United States and Canada, *al-Ittihad,* iv/2 (1968), p. 3.

6 Muslim Students Association of the United States and Canada, *al-Ittihad,* iii/2 (1966), p. 35.

7 Edward E. Curtis (ed.), *Encyclopedia of Muslim-American History* (New York, 2010), p. 572.

8 Mattson radio interview in 2007 with Krista Tippett for 'On Being', recorded at Minnesota Public Radio and broadcast across the United States. See http://being.publicradio.org/programs/newvoice/transcript.shtml (accessed 14 July 2014).

9 Mattson on-stage interview with Patty Satalia, for Penn State Public Broadcasting's 'Common Ground Lobby Talk', co-sponsored by Penn State Institute for the Arts and Humanities. See http://www.youtube.com/watch?v=LXzPV2G5PFg (accessed 14 July 2014).

10 John Mintz and Douglas Farah, 'In Search of Friends Among the Foes,' *Washington Post,* 11 September 2004, p. A1.

11 Abdullah Yusuf Ali, *The Meaning of the Glorious Quran* (Lahore, 1934), p. 54. See http://quranexplorer.com/index/Sura_004_An_Nisa_WOMEN. aspx (accessed 14 July 2014).

12 Abdullah Saeed, *The Qur'an: An Introduction*, Routledge, New York, 2008, p. 132. See also www.sublimequran.org/translations (accessed 14 July 2014).

13 Sheila Musaji, 'Laleh Bakhtiar's Qur'an Translation Controversy Over Verse 4:34', *American Muslim* (online magazine), 25 October 2007. See also www. sublimequran.org/2007/10/26/isna-presidents-message-of-support (accessed 25 August 2014).

14 See www.youtube.com/watch?v=scFUKFk01lw (accessed 14 July 2014).

15 Don Terry, 'W. Deen Mohammed: A Leap of Faith', *Chicago Tribune*, 20 October 2002, p. 1. Available at www.chicagotribune.com/news/chi-021020 -mohammedprofile,0,1786949,full.story (accessed 14 July 2014).

16 See www.youtube.com/watch?v=FvEabk4KxR0&NR=1 (accessed 14 July 2014).

17 Ilyas Ba-Yunus and Kassim Kone, *Muslims in the United States* (Westport, CT, 2006), p. 25.

18 Ibid., p. 52.

19 Ibid.

20 Julie Pasternal, 'The Imam's Next Move', *Los Angeles Times*, 4 August 1994. Available at http://articles.latimes.com/1994-08-04/news/ls-332 84_1_w-deen-mohammed (accessed 14 July 2014).

5. The Shock of 9/11

1 Laurie Goodstein, 'U.S. Muslim Clerics Seek a Moderate Middle Ground', *New York Times*, 18 June 2006, p. 1.

2 Mark Steyn, *America Alone: The End of the World as we Know it* (Washington, DC, 2006).

3 Gallup Center for Muslim Studies, 'Religious Perceptions in America: With an In-Depth Analysis of U.S. Attitudes Toward Muslims and Islam', 21 January 2010. See www.gallup.com/poll/125312/religious-prejudice-stronger-against-muslims.aspx (accessed 14 July 2014).

4 'Fire Set at Mosque Where Terror Suspect Worshiped', *USA Today* (online edition), 29 November 2010. Available at www.usatoday.com/news/nation/ 2010-11-28-Arson-Oregon_N.htm (accessed 14 July 2014).

5 Michael d'Oliveira, 'Lauderhill Commission Tables Islamic Center Resolution', *Sun Sentinel* (website of Orlando Sun Sentinel), 15 December 2010. Available at http://articles.sun-sentinel.com/2010-12-15/news/fl-tf-park51-1208-20101215_1_lauderhill-commission-islamic-center-resolution (accessed 14 July 2014).

6 Stephanie Condon, 'Palin's "Refudiate" Tweet on Mosque Near Ground Zero Draws Fire (for Substance and Style)', 19 July 2010, *CBS News* (online). Available at www.cbsnews.com/news/palins-refudiate-tweet-on-mosque-near-ground-zero-draws-fire-for-substance-and-style (accessed 14 July 2014).

7 Andy Ostroy, 'What's Truly at Stake in the Ground Zero Mosque Debate', 17 August 2010, *Huffington Post* (online). Available at www.huffingtonpost.

com/andy-ostroy/whats-truly-at-stake-in-t_b_684511.html (accessed 25 August 2014).

8 Richard Allen Greene, 'U.S. Muslims Underestimate 9/11 Effect, Muslim Thinker Warns', belief blog, CNN (online), 5 August 2010. See http://religion. blogs.cnn.com/2010/08/05/u-s-muslims-underestimate-911-effect-muslim-thinker-warns (accessed 14 July 2014).

9 Pew Research Center, *Muslim Americans: Middle Class and Mostly Mainstream* (Washington, DC, 2007), p. 41.

10 Ibid., p. 37.

11 Ibid., p. 42.

12 Ibid., p. 59.

13 See www.youtube.com/watch?v=3IofpsHOosE (accessed 14 July 2014).

14 Judith Miller, 'The Afghans of Fremont: Anxious, Uprooted – and Under Surveillance', *City Journal*, xx/4 (Autumn 2010). Available at www.city-journal.org/2010/20_4_fremont-ca-afghans.html (accessed 14 July 2014).

15 A.G. Sulzberger and William K. Rashbaum, 'Guilty Plea Made in Plot to Bomb New York Subway', *New York Times*, 23 February 2010, p. A1. Available at www.nytimes.com/2010/02/23/nyregion/23terror.html?_r=0 (accessed 14 July 2014).

16 Fawaz Gerges, *The Rise and Fall of al-Qaeda* (New York, 2011), p. 156.

17 Ibid., p. 164.

6. The Diversity of American Muslims

1 Pew Research Center, *Muslim Americans: Middle Class and Mostly Mainstream* (Washington, DC, 2007), p. 11.

2 Ibid., p. 15.

3 Ibid.

4 Ibid.

5 Ibid.

6 Ibid., p. 17.

7 Ibid., p. 22.

8 Ibid., p. 17.

9 Ibid.

10 Ibid., p. 21.

11 Ibid.

12 Ibid.

13 Gallup, *Muslim Americans: A National Portrait* (Washington, DC, 2009), p. 21.

14 Ibid.

15 Ibid., p. 20.

16 Ibid.

17 John Zogby, 'Muslims in the American Public Square: Shifting Political Winds & Fallout from 9/11, Afghanistan and Iraq' (Washington, DC, 2004), p. 3.

18 Ibid.

19 MAPS (Muslims in the American Public Square)/Zogby International, 'American Muslim Poll', November/December 2001. See www.roper center. uconn.edu/public-perspective/ppscan/134/134017.pdf, p. 42 (accessed 25 August 2014).
20 Pew Research Center, *Muslim Americans: Middle Class and Mostly Mainstream*, p. 10.
21 Ibid.
22 Ihsan Bagby, *The American Mosque 2011: Report Number 1 from the US Mosque Study 2011* (n.p., 2012), p. 4.
23 Zahid Hussain Bukhari (ed.), *Muslims' Place in the American Public Square: Hope, Fears, and Aspirations* (Walnut Creek, CA, 2004), p. 300.
24 Barry A. Kosmin and Ariela Keysar, *American Religious Identification Survey* (Hartford, CT, 2009), p. 5.
25 Ibid.
26 See Frank Newport, 'Religious Identity: States Differ Widely', Gallup, 7 August 2009. Available at www.gallup.com/poll/122075/religious-identity-states-differ-widely.aspx (accessed 14 July 2014).
27 Kosmin and Keysar, *American Religious Identification Survey*, p. 5.
28 Pew Forum on Religion & Public Life, *U.S. Religious Landscape Survey* (Washington, DC, 2008), p. 21.
29 Bagby, *The American Mosque 2011*, p. 5.
30 Ibid., p. 4.
31 Ibid., p. 6.
32 Ibid., p. 13.
33 Ibid., p. 14.
34 Ibid., p. 7.
35 Pew Research Center, *Muslim Americans: Middle Class and Mostly Mainstream*, p. 22.
36 Ibid.
37 Ibid., p. 21.
38 Ibid., p. 22.
39 Raymond Brady Williams, *Religions of Immigrants from India and Pakistan: New Threads in the American Tapestry* (New York, 1988), p. 211.
40 'Embodying Ethics, Performing Pluralism: Volunteerism Among Ismailis in Houston, TX', The Pluralism Project at Harvard University, 2003. Available at http://pluralism.org/reports/view/200 (accessed 14 July 2014).
41 Edward E. Curtis (ed.), *Encyclopedia of Muslim-American History* (New York, 2010), pp. 114, 361, 416, 475, 536.
42 Jonathan Curiel, 'Poet Follows his own Muse in Translating Sufi Mystic', *San Francisco Chronicle*, 4 August 2002, p. D4.
43 See the group's website at http://nurashkijerrahi.org (accessed 14 July 2014).
44 Neil MacFarquhar, 'Nation of Islam at a Crossroad as Leader Exits', *New York Times*, 26 February 2007, p. A1.
45 Leslie M. Alexander and Walter C. Rucker (eds), *Encyclopedia of African American History* (Santa Barbara, CA, 2010), p. 613.

46 Pamela Constable, 'Va. Mosque Vandalism Draws Sympathy for Long-Persecuted Muslim Sect', *Washington Post*, 20 February 2012.
47 Richard Brent Turner, *Islam in the African-American Experience* (Bloomington, IN, 2003), p. 130.
48 Pew Research Center, 'Muslim Americans: No Signs of Growth in Alienation or Support for Extremism', August 2011, p. 68.
49 Ibid., p. 4.
50 Bagby, *The American Mosque 2011*, p. 11.
51 Curtis, *Encyclopedia of Muslim-American History*, p. 572.
52 National Commission on Terrorist Attacks Upon the United States, *The 9/11 Commission Report*, 22 July 2004, pp. 216, 222.
53 Zogby, 'Muslims in the American Public Square', p. 3.
54 Pew Research Center, *Muslim Americans: Middle Class and Mostly Mainstream*, p. 15.
55 Arab American Institute, 'Demographics'. Available at www.aaiusa.org/pages/demographics (accessed 14 July 2014).
56 Ibid.
57 Ibid.
58 G. Patricia de la Cruz and Angela Brittingham, 'The Arab Population: 2000,' United States Census Bureau, issued December 2003, p. 5. Available at www.census.gov/prod/2003pubs/c2kbr-23.pdf (accessed 25 August 2014).
59 Pew Research Center, *Muslim Americans: Middle Class and Mostly Mainstream*, p. 22.
60 Zogby, 'Muslims in the American Public Square', p. 3.
61 Pew Research Center, *Muslim Americans: Middle Class and Mostly Mainstream*, p. 15.
62 Ibid.
63 Ibid., p. 19.
64 Ibid., p. 15.
65 Ibid., p. 22.
66 Zogby, 'Muslims in the American Public Square', p. 3.
67 Pew Research Center, *Muslim Americans: Middle Class and Mostly Mainstream*, p. 1.
68 Zogby, 'Muslims in the American Public Square', p. 45.
69 Bagby, *The American Mosque 2011*, p. 12.
70 Pew Research Center, *Muslim Americans: Middle Class and Mostly Mainstream*, p. 22.
71 Ibid.
72 Ibid., p. 17.
73 The Pew study estimates there are 1.4 million American Muslims, with Hispanics representing 4 percent of the population, or a total of 56,000.
74 Ibid., p. 24.
75 Ibid.
76 Ibid., p. 25.
77 Ibid., p. 85.

78   Institution for the Secularization of Islamic Society, 'Statement of Principles'. Available at www.centerforinquiry.net/isis/about (accessed 14 July 2014).
79   Institution for the Secularization of Islamic Society, 'Practical Goals'. Available at www.centerforinquiry.net/isis/about/practical_goals (accessed 14 July 2014).
80   Laurie Goodstein, 'Stereotyping Rankles Silent, Secular Majority of American Muslims', *New York Times*, 23 December 2001, p. A20.
81   Gallup, *Muslim Americans: A National Portrait*, p. 32.
82   Michelangelo Signorile, 'Internet Innovators', *Advocate*, 14 March 2000, p. 27.
83   David Morton Rayside and Clyde Wilcox, *Faith, Politics, and Sexual Diversity in Canada and the United States* (Vancouver, BC, 2011), p. 271.
84   Will O'Bryan, 'A Man for All Seasons: Imam Daayiee Abduallah Offers a Gay Muslim's Insights for the Holidays', *Metro Weekly*, 21 December 2006.
85   Barry A. Kosmin, Egon Mayer, and Ariela Keysar, *American Religious Identification Survey, 2001* (New York, 2001), pp. 39–42.
86   Gallup, *Muslim Americans: A National Portrait,* p. 132.
87   Ibid., p. 28.
88   Ibid., p. 29.
89   Zogby, 'Muslims in the American Public Square', p. 44.
90   Bagby, *The American Mosque 2011*, p. 7.
91   Pew Research Center, *Muslim Americans: Middle Class and Mostly Mainstream*, p. 24.
92   Ibid., p. 23.
93   Ibid., p. 33.
94   Ibid., p. 2.
95   Ibid., p. 89.
96   Ibid., p. 31.
97   Ibid., p. 87.
98   Ibid., p. 34.
99   Vartan Gregorian, *Islam: A Mosaic, Not a Monolith* (Washington, DC, 2003), p. viii.
100   Ibid., p. 3.

7. Who's Who in Muslim America

1   Mike Ghouse, 'Hate Sermons: Nonie Darwish; a Hate Monger', HateSermons.Blogspot.com, 9 August 2009. Available at http://hatesermons. blogspot.com/2009/08/nonie-darwish-hate-monger.html (accessed 14 July 2014).
2   Sally Quinn, 'The God Vote: Akbar Ahmed on Terrorism and American Islam', *Washington Post* (online), 12 February 2010. Available at www.washing tonpost.com/wp-dyn/content/video/2010/12/02/VI2010120203565.html (accessed 14 July 2014).
3   Hana Yasmeen Ali, interview with Deborah Caldwell, Beliefnet, February 2005. Available at www.beliefnet.com/Faiths/Islam/2005/02/Muhammad-Alis-New-Spiritual-Quest.aspx?p=1 (accessed 14 July 2014).

4   Ibid.
5   Ali interview with ITV Sports Channel, 1977. Available at www.youtube. com/watch?v=x7YF58ygric (accessed 14 July 2014).
6   Ibid.
7   Asad Hashim, 'Imam on a Mission,' blogs.aljazeera.net, 9 June 2011. Available at http://blogs.aljazeera.net/americas/2011/09/06/imam-mission (accessed 14 July 2014).
8   Author interview with Aslan at the Commonwealth Club of California, 1 September 2009. Available at http://commonwealthclub.blogspot.com/ 2009/09/reza-aslan-no-clash-of-civilizations.html (accessed 14 July 2014).
9   Keith Gottschalk, Blogcritics.org, 8 April 2005. Available at http://blogcritics. org/books/article/interview-reza-aslan-author-no-god/page-6/ (accessed 14 July 2014).
10 Khaled Abou El Fadl, *The Great Theft: Wrestling Islam from the Extremists* (New York, 2005), p. 4.
11 Niraj Warikoo, 'Ellison Says Faith Won't Be Exploited', *Detroit Free Press*, 28 December 2006.
12 Douglas A. Hicks, *With God on All Sides: Leadership in a Devout and Diverse America* (New York, 2009), p. xvii.
13 Kabbani interview: 'Muhammad Hisham Kabbani: "The Muslim Experience in America is Unprecedented"', *Middle East Quarterly* vii/2, 2000, pp. 61–72. Available at www.meforum.org/61/muhammad-hisham-kabbani-the-muslim-experience-in (accessed 14 July 2014).
14 Knight blogged at http://knight.progressiveislam.org. His blog ended on 14 July 2006. For the cited blog post, see http://web.archive.org/ web/20060203052709/http://knight.progressiveislam.org/?p=4 (accessed 14 July 2014).
15 Poems posted on 23 September 2010 at www.cagedprisoners.com. See www. cageprisoners.com/our-work/alerts/item/611-update-john-walker-lindh (accessed 14 July 2014).
16 See www.cageprisoners.com/learn-more/for-the-victims/item/609-ode-to-omar-khadr (accessed 14 July 2014).
17 See www.galaxy.com/rvw968365-620145/Www-freejohnwalker-net.htm and www.causes.com/causes/178868-president-obama-free-john-walker-lindh/ about (accessed 25 August 2014).
18 Ingrid Mattson, 'Heaven's Gate: How Muslim Women Open and Close Doors for their Sisters', Macdonald Center for the Study of Islam and Christian–Muslim Relations, Hartford Seminary website, p. 61. Available at http://ingridmattson.org/article/heavens-gate-how-muslim-women-open-or-close-doors-for-their-sisters (accessed 25 August 2014).
19 Mattson, 'Heaven's Gate', p. 67.
20 Interview with Mehdi Hasan of the *New Statesman*: 'Dalia Mogahed – Extended Interview', *New Statesman*, 12 February 2010. Available at www. newstatesman.com/religion/2010/02/interview-obama-muslim (accessed 14 July 2014).

21 Qazwini's speech posted on his website, 1 October 2003, see http://alqa zwini.org/qazwini_org/news/news_page/news_100103.htm (accessed 14 July 2014).

22 Feisal Abdul Rauf, *What's Right with Islam is What's Right with America* (New York, 2004), p. 230.

23 Paul Vitello, 'Imam Behind Islamic Center Plans U.S. Tour', *New York Times*, 24 December 2010, p. A18.

24 Zaid Shakir, *Scattered Pictures: Reflections of an American Muslim* (Hayward, CA, 2005), p. 21.

25 Jonathan Curiel, 'Muslim Comics Sway Believers, Nonbelievers as they Poke Clean Fun at Life, Policies in U.S.', *San Francisco Chronicle*, 19 October 2004, p. E1.

26 Amina Wadud, *Inside the Gender Jihad: Women's Reform in Islam,* (Oxford, 2006), p. viii.

27 Suhaib Webb, 'Convert Removing Tattoo', 8 January 2012. Available at www.suhaibwebb.com/islam-studies/faqs-and-fatwas/convert-removing-tattoo (accessed 14 July 2014).

28 Omar Sacirbey, 'A New Imam, a New Outlook: Leader of Roxbury Mosque Says he Brings a Welcoming Vision', *Boston Globe,* 3 December 2011, p. B1.

29 John Esposito and Ibrahim Kalin (eds), *The 500 Most Influential Muslims: 2009* (Amman, Jordan, 2009), p. 29.

30 Jack O'Sullivan, 'If you Hate the West, Emigrate to a Muslim Country', *Guardian*, 7 October 2001, p. I11.

31 Rafia Zakaria, 'Reform or Renounce?: Ayaan Hirsi Ali and Muslim Women', *Guernica*, 15 June 2010. Available at www.guernicamag.com/blog/1835/ rafia_zakaria_reform_or_renoun (accessed 14 July 2014).

32 Neil MacFarquhar, 'For Muslim Students on Inclusion', *New York Times*, 28 February 2008, p. A14.

33 'The Sufis – Enlightened Community Builders', Islamic Supreme Council of America website. Available at www.islamicsupremecouncil.org/ understanding-islam/spirituality/2-the-sufis-enlightened-community-builders.html (accessed 14 July 2014).

34 'About us', Islamic Supreme Council of America website. Available at www. islamicsupremecouncil.org/home/about-us.html (accessed 14 July 2014).

35 'AIC's Story', American Islamic Congress website. Available at www. aicongress.org/aboutaic/aicstory (accessed 14 July 2014).

36 Nawab Agha, Omran Salman, Kemal Silay, Stephen Suleyman Schwartz, Salim Mansur, Jalal Zuberi, Imaad Malik, M. Zuhdi Jasser, and Sheikh Ahmed Subhy Mansour, 'Attention Rabbi Yoffie: Please Speak to Moderate Muslims', *Jewish Week*, 2 June 2008. Available at www.islamicpluralism. org/575/attention-rabbi-yoffie-please-speak-to-moderate-muslims (accessed 14 July 2014).

37 'Resolution', *As-Sabiqun* (online newsletter), November 1995, p. 2. Available online at http://nebula.wsimg.com/5afd8d7d7bfea0f7f5e7a88a9c9ff28a? AccessKeyId=7BF28DA361146B27EBBEdisposition=0&alloworigin=1 (accessed 25 August 2014). See p. 2.

38 'Urgent Appeal', As-Sabiqun blog site, 21 January 2011. Available at http://
    sabiqundc.blogspot.com/2011/01/urgent-appeal.html (accessed 14 July
    2014).

8. Gender and Religion

1 Robert Polner, 'Prayers and Protest', *Newsday*, 18 March 2005.
2 'Islamic Thinkers Society Crash Amina Wadud Women Led Prayer', 16 May
   2009. Available at www.youtube.com/watch?v=2TQ68mm3WB8 (accessed
   14 July 2014). For information on the Islamic Thinkers, see www.youtube.
   com/user/islamicthinkers (accessed 14 July 2014).
3 'Islamic Thinkers Society Crash Amina Wadud Women Led Prayer'.
4 Elli Safari, *The Noble Struggle of Amina Wadud*, 2007, Netherlands/
   United States, 29 minutes. Available at www.webislam.com/videos/
   56727-documental_sobre_amina_wadud_en_ingles.html (accessed 14 July
   2014).
5 Nomani's 'Islamic Bill of Rights' was published as an appendix in her book,
   Standing Alone: An American Woman's Struggle for the Soul of Islam (New York,
   2006), p. 293. Also available on the Beliefnet.com website at www.beliefnet.
   com/Faiths/Islam/2005/06/The-Islamic-Bill-Of-Rights-For-Women-In-
   Mosques.aspx (accessed 14 July 2014).
6 Jonathan Curiel, 'Muslim Women Rip Veil off Religion's Traditional Gender
   Values', *San Francisco Chronicle*, 28 August 2005, p. F1.
7 Asra Nomani, 'Let these Women Pray!', *Daily Beast*, 27 February 2001.
   Available at www.thedailybeast.com/articles/2010/02/27/let-these-women-
   pray.html (accessed 14 July 2014).
8 Ibid.
9 Ihsan Bagby, Paul M. Perl, and Bryan T. Froehle, *The Mosque in America: A
   National Portrait* (Washington, DC, 2001), p. 56.
10 Ibid., p. 11.
11 Ibid.
12 *Women Friendly Mosques and Community Centers: Working Together to Reclaim
   our Heritage* was published as a PDF in 2005, by Women in Islam, Inc.,
   and Islamic Social Services Assocations, and supported by the Council on
   American-Islamic Relations – Canada, the Islamic Circle of North America, the
   Islamic Society of North America, the Muslim Alliance in North America, the
   Muslim Association of Canada, and MSA-Canada. See www.islamawareness.
   net/Mosque/WomenAndMosquesBooklet.pdf (accessed 25 August 2014).
13 Ibid., p. 8.
14 Ibid., p. 11.
15 Andrea Useem, 'Does the Qu'ran Tolerate Domestic Abuse?', Beliefnet, July
   2007. Available at www.beliefnet.com/Faiths/Islam/2007/07/Does-The-
   Quran-Tolerate-Domestic-Abuse.aspx (accessed 14 July 2014).
16 Safari, *The Noble Struggle of Amina Wadud*.
17 See Asma Barlas, 'Islam, Women and Equality', p. 2, Asma Barlas website.
   Available at www.asmabarlas.com/EDITORIALS/IslamWomenII.pdf (accessed 14 July 2014).

18 Fons Elders, 'Islam (part 1)', commissioned by Dutch Islamic Broadcast Nederlandse Islamitische Omroep, posted on YouTube, 30 November 2009. Available at www.youtube.com/watch?v=g6SmQyl4dAY (accessed 14 July 2014).

19 Ibid.

20 Mona Eltahawy, 'Meanwhile: Making History at Friday Prayer', *New York Times*, 29 March 2005. Available at www.nytimes.com/2005/03/28/opinion/28iht-edeltahawy.html (accessed 25 August 2014).

21 Wadud, *Inside the Gender Jihad*, p. 96.

9. In Politics, Muslim-Americans Progress One Step at a Time

1 Bruce Nichols, 'Front-Runner in Council Race Builds on Growing Ethnic Clout', *Dallas Morning News*, 23 November 2003.

2 The consulate general of Pakistan in Houston estimates that the number of Pakistani-Americans in the Houston area is 100,000. See www.pakistanconsulatehouston.org/localcom.asp (accessed 14 July 2014). According to US census data from 2010, 409,163 Pakistani-American immigrants live in the United States (Asian American Center for Advancing Justice, 'A Community of Contrasts: Asian Americans in the United States: 2011' (n.p., n.d.), p. 11). In 2008, researchers at the Migration Policy Institute, a think tank in Washington, DC, estimated that the greater Houston area was home to 7.4 percent of all Pakistani-Americans (see www.migrationinformation.org/USFocus/display.cfm?ID=672 (accessed 14 July 2014)). And in 2001, the *Houston Chronicle* said about 60,000 Pakistani-Americans lived in the Houston area: 'Pakistani-Americans Blend into Daily Life in the Land of Opportunity', *Houston Chronicle*, 28 October 2001, p. 1.

3 Based on 2010 census figures, see http://factfinder2.census. gov/faces/tableservices/jsf/pages/productview.xhtml?pid=ACS_11_5YR_DP02&prodType=table and www.census.gov/fastfacts (accessed 14 July 2014).

4 Based on 2009–11 census figures. See http://www.fns.usda.gov/sites/default/files/ops/Indiana_7.pdf (accessed 25 August 2014).

5 Gallup, *Muslim Americans: A National Portrait* (Washington, DC, 2009) p. 70.

6 Emma Brown, 'Mukit Hossain, Muslim Activist in Northern Virginia, Dies', *Washington Post*, 28 November 2010, p. B4.

7 'American Muslims Overwhelmingly Backed Obama', *Newsweek*, 6 November 2008. Available at www.newsweek.com/american-muslims-overwhelmingly-backed-obama-85173 (accessed 25 August 2014).

8 William Saletan, 'Islam is Ground Zero', *Slate*, 16 August 2010. Available at www.slate.com/articles/news_and_politics/frame_game/2010/08/islam_is_ground_zero.html (accessed 14 July 2014).

9 Nick Wing, 'Keith Ellison, Muslim Congressman, Says "Ground Zero Mosque" Foes Are Birther-Types, "Proponents of Religious Bigotry"', *Huffington Post*, 7 September 2010. Available at www.huffington post.com/2010/09/07/keith-ellison-muslim-cong_n_707593.html (accessed 14 July 2014).

10   Jeremy Herb, 'Ellison: There's Room for Islamic Center Near Ground
       Zero', *Star Tribune*, 14 September 2010. Available at www.startribune.com/
       templates/Print_This_Story?sid=102820094 (accessed 14 July 2014).
11   Mitch Anderson, 'Ellison: Hajj Was Transformative', *Star Tribune*,
       18 December 2008. Available at www.startribune.com/printarticle/
       ?id=36417549 (accessed 14 July 2014).
12   Ibid.
13   Kevin Diaz, 'Islamic Nonprofit Paid for Rep. Ellison's Pilgrimage to Mecca',
       Star Tribune, 22 July 2009. Available at www.startribune.com/templates/
       Print_This_Story?sid=51361722 (accessed 14 July 2014).
14   Lance Gay, 'Muslim Delegates Uneasy in Bush's America', *American Muslim
       Perspective*, 27 July 2004. Available at www.ampolitics.ghazali.net/html/
       muslim_delegates.html (accessed 14 July 2014).
15   Ibid.
16   Ben Smith, 'Muslims Barred from Photo at Obama Event', *Politco*, published
       on *USA Today*'s website, 18 June 2008. Available at www.faithstreet.com/
       onfaith/2008/10/19/powell-rejects-islamophobia/103 (accessed 14 July
       2014).
17   Abed Z. Bhuyan, 'Powell Rejects Islamaphobia', *Washington Post*, 19
       October 2008. Available at http://onfaith.washingtonpost.com/onfaith/
       guestvoices/2008/10/powell_rejects_islamophobia.html.
18   Michael Laris, 'Saqib Ali Sidesteps "Muslim Candidate" Label in Race for
       Maryland Senate', *Washington Post*, 10 September 2010. Available at www.
       washingtonpost.com/wp-dyn/content/article/2010/09/09/AR2010090906
       939.html (accessed 14 July 2014).
19   Edward Hegstrom, 'Area's Diversity Represented', *Houston Chronicle*, 22
       December 2003, p. 22.
20   Ibid.
21   Ibid.
22   Laris, 'Saqib Ali Sidesteps "Muslim Candidate" Label'.

10. Conflicts and Co-Existence

1   Terrence Stutz, 'Texas Board of Education OKs Resolution Against Pro-
      Islamic References in Textbooks', *Dallas Morning News*, 24 September 2010.
      Available at www.dallasnews.com/news/education/headlines/20100924-
      Texas-Board-of-Education-OKs-resolution-9609.ece (accessed 14 July
      2014).
2   Brian Thevenot, 'SBOE Conservatives Allege Islamic Bias in Textbooks',
      Texas Tribune, 15 September 2010. Available at www.texastribune.org/texas-
      education/state-board-of-education/sboe-conservatives-allege-islamic-bias-
      in-books (accessed 14 July 2014).
3   Qazwini's speech on 1 October 2010 at the Islamic Center of America. See
      the speech at www.youtube.com/watch? v=R9Gf46WnFxc& feature=player_
      embedded (accessed 14 July 2014).
4   Pew Research Center, *Muslim Americans: Middle Class and Mostly Mainstream*
      (Washington, DC, 2007), p. 90.

5   Ihsan Bagby, Paul M. Perl, and Bryan T. Froehle, *The Mosque in America: A National Portrait* (Washington, DC, 2001), p. 11.
6   Comment by 'Intellect' to story by Annie Minoff, 'Snapshots from the Muslim-Punk Underground', Studio360.org, 24 July 2009. Available at www.studio360.org/blogs/studio-360-blog/2009/jul/24/snapshots-from-the-muslim-punk-underground (accessed 14 July 2014).
7   The video 'Is Muslim Punk Rock Haram? Part 1–5' was on YouTube between 2007 and 2010, then removed, then reappeared in 2013, at www.youtube.com/watch?v=dROPwJF_O9Y (accessed 25 August 2014).
8   Scott Collins and Matea Gold, 'Threat Against "South Park" Creators Highlights Dilemma for Media Companies', *Los Angeles Times*, 23 April 2010. Available at http://articles.latimes.com/2010/apr/23/entertainment/la-et-south-park-20100423 (accessed 14 July 2014).
9   Associated Press, 'Dalai Lama Meets with Muslims, Urges Religious Tolerance', *USA Today*, 16 April 2006. Available at www.usatoday.com/news/nation/2006-04-16-dalailama-muslims_x.htm (accessed 14 July 2014).
10 Pew Research Center, *Muslim Americans: Middle Class and Mostly Mainstream*, p. 15.
11 Bagby, Perl, and Froehle, *The Mosque in America: A National Portrait*, p. 23.
12 Gallup, *Muslim Americans: A National Portrait* (Washington, DC, 2009), p. 132.
13 Pew Research Center, *Muslim Americans: Middle Class and Mostly Mainstream*, p. 87.
14 Ibid.
15 Stephen Hudak, 'Gainesville Pastor Plans to Burn Islamic Holy Book Despite General's Plea', *Orlando Sentinel*, 8 September 2010. Available at http://articles.orlandosentinel.com/2010-09-08/news/os-koran-burning-20100908_1_pastor-terry-jones-dove-world-outreach-center-gainesville-pastor-plans (accessed 14 July 2014).
16 Sally Quinn, 'The God Vote: Akbar Ahmed on terrorism and American Islam,' 12 February 2010. Available at www.washingtonpost.com/wp-dyn/content/video/2010/12/02/VI2010120203565.html (accessed 14 July 2014).
17 Gallup Center for Muslim Studies, 'Religious Perceptions in America: With an In-Depth Analysis of U.S. Attitudes Toward Muslims and Islam', 21 January 2010. See p. 7 of www.gallup.com/poll/125312/religious-prejudice-stronger-against-muslims.aspx (accessed 25 August 2014).
18 Ibid.
19 Ihsan Bagby, *The American Mosque 2011: Report Number 1 from the US Mosque Study 2011* (n.p., 2012), p. 12.
20 Pew Research Center, *Muslim Americans: Middle Class and Mostly Mainstream*, p. 37.
21 Interview for Jonathan Curiel, *Al' America: Travels Through America's Arab and Islamic Roots* (New York, 2008).
22 Edward E. Curtis IV (ed.), *The Columbia Sourcebook of Muslims in the United States* (New York, 2008), p. 323.

23 Azhar Usman, 'An Apology', 2008. Available at http://dawudwalid.wordpress. com/2008/09/13/an-apology-azhar-usman (accessed 14 July 2014).

24 Ibid.

25 Bruce Lawrence, *New Faiths, Old Fears: Muslims and Other Asian Immigrants in American Religious Life* (New York, 2002), pp. 83–4.

26 Usman, 'An Apology'.

27 Jonathan Curiel, 'Muslim Comics Sway Believers, Nonbelievers as they Poke Clean Fun at Life, Policies in U.S.', *San Francisco Chronicle*, 19 October 2004.

28 Jonathan Curiel, 'Muslims in Marin: The Home of John Walker Lindh Shows its Hospitality Toward Followers of Islam', *San Francisco Chronicle*, 27 May 2007, p. E1.

29 Yvonne Yazbek Haddad (ed.), *The Muslims of America* (New York, 1991), p. 3.

30 Ibid., p. 5.

31 Fakih tweeted 'Ramadan Kareem, Blessed Month of Ramadan' on 31 July 2011, and posted on her Twitter feed, at twitter.com/#!/OfficialRima/statuses/97766340110204929. A screen shot of the tweet was taken on 23 February 2012. Several weeks later, Fakih's tweets were removed, and she announced that her Twitter feed had been 'hacked on 3/14/12'.

32 Interview for Curiel, *Al' America*.

33 Posted on the website of the Florida Family Assocation. Available at http://floridafamily.org/full_article.php?article_no=108 (accessed 14 July 2014).

34 Video posted on the website of the *Hollywood Reporter*, to accompany a story on the controversy, by Erin Carlson, 'Jon Stewart Skews TLC, Lowe's Over "American Muslim" Boycott', 14 December 2011. Available at www.hollywoodreporter.com/news/jon-stewart-lowes-american-muslim-273664 (accessed 14 July 2014).

35 S. Abdallah Schleifer (ed.), *The 500 Most Influential Muslims, 2011*, (Amman, Jordan, 2011), p. 143.

36 Daniel Massey, 'Web-Inspired Parade Protest: Florida-Based Group Says City's Muslim Day Event Is a "Threat," Prompting Barrage of Phone Calls, Letters and E-Mails to City Hall', *Newsday*, 8 September 2007.

Select Bibliography

Alford, Terry, *Prince Among Slaves: The True Story of an African Prince Sold into Slavery in the American South* (New York, 1977).

Austin, Allan D., *African Muslims in Antebellum America* (New York, 1997).

—— *African Muslims in Antebellum America: A Sourcebook* (New York, 1984).

Bagby, Ihsan, *The American Mosque 2011: Report Number 1 from the US Mosque Study 2011* (n.p., 2012).

Bagby, Ihsan, Paul M. Perl, and Bryan T. Froehle, *The Mosque in America: A National Portrait* (Washington, DC, 2001).

Bluett, Thomas, *Some Memories of the Life of Job, the Son of the Solomon High Priest of Boonda in Africa; Who was a Slave about Two Years in Maryland; and Afterwards Being Brought to England, Was Set Free, and Sent to his Native Land in the Year 1734* (London, 1734).

Curtis, Edward E. (ed.), *Encyclopedia of Muslim American History* (New York, 2010).

—— *Muslims in America: A Short History* (New York, 2009).

GhaneaBassiri, Kambiz, *A History of Islam in America: From the New World to the New World Order* (New York, 2010).

Gomez, Michael A., *Black Crescent: The Experience and Legacy of African Muslims in the Americas* (New York, 2005).

Pew Research Center, *Muslim Americans: Middle Class and Mostly Mainstream* (Washington, DC, 2007).

Wadud, Amina, *Inside the Gender Jihad: Women's Reform in Islam* (Oxford, 2006).

Index